LIVING
WITH LONG-TERM ILLNESS

Nina Kaye

For every person with chronic illness – you deserve a better life.

Preface

There are hundreds of millions of people across the world who are struggling with long-term (chronic) illness. They are one of the most overlooked and vulnerable groups in society, who in addition to their health challenges can face unfair criticism, accusations of faking, prejudice and stigma. I am one of them.

In 2013, my body began to malfunction in a confusing and terrifying way. By summer 2014, I could barely walk, I had continuous pronounced bodily tremors, my speech, hearing and sight were affected, I was severely breathless and fatigued, and I was experiencing several episodes of uncontrollable shaking and muscle spasms every day. And that was only part of the picture.

Though every person's experience will be different, there are common themes that chime with familiarity for people with long-term illnesses: loneliness, a sense of isolation, helplessness, hopelessness, loss of control over one's life, loss of independence, feeling useless or forgotten about, not feeling believed or listened to and stigmatisation. You only have to read a news article on the topic or have a dig around online to see these themes coming through. And for every rare and astonishing success story of someone who has 'beaten the odds' and 'overcome the impossible', there are many more people living lives that offer them little to look forward to.

I have fought my way back from almost total incapacitation and learned how to LIVE with long-term illness. Living isn't just about your heart beating or taking a breath. It's about feeling alive, having a sense of purpose, having some level of contentment and fulfilment, about thinking there's a point to your existence. My way of LIVING has included returning to my career in HR, as well as becoming a published author of seven novels, a children's book and now this one. Part of my 'recovery' has come from medical interventions and medication, but a significant aspect has been to do with how I've dealt with my illness and taken the reins with my situation.

I am not someone who has 'beaten the odds'. I still live with the limitations of my condition every day, but I have built a meaningful quality of life for myself, and I want to help others do the same.

Writing this non-fiction book felt like a calling – something I had to do.

However, when I tried to find a literary agent specialising in non-fiction to represent me to publishers, the rejections from those I'd written to came quickly. They were kind and encouraging, but none were willing to take me and my book on. I had been warned this might happen: I'm not a celebrity, and I don't have a large social-media following.

I understand the commercial realities of publishing. But what saddens (or disappoints) me is that thoughtful, lived-experience voices are often sidelined simply because they aren't visible or marketable enough. People who don't seek the limelight still matter. And they still have a great deal to offer others facing similar challenges.

With that in mind, I decided to go ahead and publish this book myself, and if it only helps a handful of people then I will still consider it a success. My second novel, *Take A Moment*, which follows the life of a young woman after she receives a shock diagnosis of Multiple Sclerosis (MS), touched many of my readers with long-term illness to the point that they wrote to me to tell me about the positive impact it had on them. I'd hoped to raise awareness of chronic illness with that book and the result was better than I expected, so here I am – wanting to make more of an impact on the lives of others.

Contents

What this book is about and how to read it

Most self-help books are written by experts. They are perhaps medically trained, they might have impressive academic credentials and a string of letters after their names, or they might have become a subject matter expert through their chosen career path. Generally, they will have a deep understanding of the theory or subject matter they cover, and they will perhaps have undertaken research and/or successfully helped many people (or patients if they are medically trained). They then bring all this knowledge, expertise and experience together to present their arguments, opinions and advice in a way that is useful to the reader.

Memoirs tell a story and reflect upon it. They take us on a journey with the writer. One of discovery and reflection – on both their part and ours. They are a window into the lives of others, typically celebrities or important public figures.

I am neither an expert (in the sense of the definition above) or a notable public figure – and I'm certainly not a celebrity. What I am is a person with significant lived experience of long-term illness (an expert in that, you might say), a background in Human Resources (with a special interest in emotional intelligence, behaviours, change and personal development), and thankfully, the ability to write (though I normally write fiction or content related to my day job).

So why would you want to hear from me?

Because, in my (humble) opinion, my lived experience is just as important as the theory, arguments and advice presented in the self-help books I've described above. The more formal experts who write these books have a lot to offer (and I will talk about one who has had a big impact on me), but what they can't understand – especially when it comes to long-term illness – is how you *feel*. Not properly. Not in the way that someone with raw lived experience can – unless they have similar personal experience themselves. And if they haven't experienced long-term illness, they cannot truly understand the challenges of having a debilitating condition while trying to find your way in a society that is, in the main, set up for survival of the fittest.

I have a story to tell that I believe others with long-term illness will connect with, about the challenges I've faced and how I've worked hard to reclaim some quality of life. And about how my aforementioned 'special interest in emotional intelligence, behaviours, change and personal development' in my job has extended into to my personal life in a way that has benefitted my quality of life with my illness.

I believe that, when you're experiencing chronic illness and/or pain, it's important to know that you're not alone. That's the very reason why support groups exist and this book serves a similar purpose – sharing my experiences and learnings to help others feel less isolated. It is also my opinion (and experience) that quality of life is not prioritised in the way that survival is. There's less in the way of research into conditions that are hugely debilitating but not degenerative or life-threatening, meaning there's less treatment and support available. And on the face of it, that's the right call. We absolutely want to save people who might otherwise die from horrible diseases. I'm not saying it's an either/or situation. But, as I pointed out in the *Preface*, quality of life is also very important.

I have experienced what it's like to have almost no quality of life and it's an awful place to be. I was told, 'If you allow yourself to become an invalid, you will become an invalid'. Those words stuck with me so hard and fast, I fought back with everything I had, and while I still live with challenging symptoms and physical limitations, I am LIVING, not just drawing breath every day. This book is about helping you to do the same.

The condition I have, which you'll learn a bit about later, is highly stigmatised. This stigma adds to what is already a complex and difficult life situation because of the broad range of symptoms I experience. Which brings me to a couple of other reasons why I felt able to write this book. Firstly, while I can't pretend that I understand how every different illness feels for every individual person, I have spent time with people with a range of different long-term conditions and there are many areas of overlap and common concern, both generally and in relation to quality of life. Secondly, because I do have such a vast range of symptoms that affect me day to day, I believe that many people with long-term illness will be able to relate to my experiences in some way or another.

Being open and up front, here are the main ones (in no particular order). I don't experience them all at once. Some of them are constant, others come as part of acute flare ups of my condition.

Physical symptoms

- Chronic and acute pain (including facial pain, extreme tenderness in my upper torso and intense burning pain in my extremities)

- Fatigue and breathlessness

- Feeling weak, shaky and sick

- Muscle and joint pain and stiffness

- Severe PMS

- Headaches

- Gastrointestinal issues

- Episodes of violent shaking, tremors and muscle spasms throughout my entire body (seizure-like attacks)

- Localised tremors, involuntary movements and muscle spasms

- Problems with my fine motor skills (which can make tasks such as tying my shoelaces difficult)

- Speech issues

- Difficulty walking/my legs giving way

Cognitive/Sensory symptoms

- Short term memory problems and 'brain blanks'

- Brain fog and being unable to think straight

- Problems with my concentration – including difficulty with reading and listening and difficulty taking in the spoken word

- Problems with word finding and some areas of problem solving

- Increased pain sensitivity

- Over-reactive reflexes

- A strange tremulous feeling in my core

- My central nervous system being stuck in 'red alert'

- Sensory overload and issues with perception – including with my vision, hearing and experience of movement

- Problems with balance and physical co-ordination

So, what is this book? Is it a memoir? Is it self-help? The short answer is that it's a bit of both: telling and reflecting on my real-life story, drawing lessons from it and encouraging you as the reader to consider your own circumstances and make positive choices. It ultimately belongs on the self-help shelf, because the main purpose of it is to help you help yourself.

To give the long answer, I tell my story and I invite you to join me on a journey that – if you're currently experiencing extended ill health – will hopefully provide some sense of not feeling alone and give you something to think about. I cover my experiences in relation to a range of topics that I believe are relevant to quality of life when experiencing illness that has significant physical, cognitive and/or sensory impacts. These include coming to terms with being unwell, keeping a sense of independence and control, staying positive (as much as possible), learning to navigate life in a different way and dealing with the outside world.

The 'self-help' angle comes from sharing my experiences and insights and posing questions for you to reflect upon within your own specific set of circumstances. In Part Two and Part Three, there's a short section at the end of each chapter called *Food for thought*, where you'll find these self-reflection questions to consider at a time that's right for you. I don't recommend trying to tackle too many of them at once. Instead, I suggest considering the questions one chapter at time and in the order that you think will work best for you. What's of most interest to you? What do you feel most able to cope with? You can be your own compass and let your instincts guide you. There's just one caveat to that: as a new reader, make sure you start with Part One (my real-life story) so that you're able to follow the content in Parts Two and Three.

I also give advice about how to get the most from this book, and I offer examples or options where I think it could be helpful to get you thinking. However, at no point do I tell you what you should or shouldn't do in relation to your own health circumstances, because every person's experience of illness, what they can and can't cope with, and what does and doesn't work for them, is different. I simply signpost areas for you to consider *if* you want to. And that's a really important point: please read this with your own circumstances and needs in mind, not to compare your illness with mine, because even if there are areas of overlap, it won't be the same.

I've structured the main self-help content into short, easily digestible chapters that you can dip in and out of as you like. As someone who struggles with reading myself, I understand how challenging it can be to read and/or concentrate when you're unwell. For maximum benefit, I'd recommend doing this (the 'dipping in and out') regularly to help you stay focused on creating a better quality of life for yourself. This book can also act as a support tool when you're stumbling. The chapters and self-reflection questions in Part Two and Part Three are designed to be used in exactly that way.

This is also probably a good time to mention that, throughout the book, I use the labels of 'long-term illness' and 'chronic illness' interchangeably and they mean the same thing (I'm not a fan of constant repetition – you can blame the fiction author in me for that!).

Finally, I need to be *really* clear that I'm not providing medical advice of any sort, and you should always check with your doctor or specialist consultant if you're in any doubt in relation to your own personal health situation. There are things I can do that you may not be able to and it's essential that you don't put yourself at risk in any way.

If you are a reader with a long-term illness, I hope you find this book helpful, and that you will be able to take some personal insights away from it to help you LIVE. You might even be reading this book because someone close to you is unwell, in which case, please use it to gain a better understanding of what chronic illness can feel like, not to tell them how to live. Ultimately, it's for the person with the illness to decide what is and isn't right for them. Also, it takes time to break old habits and form new ones, which means that, even if your loved one wants to make changes, it won't happen overnight and they may have a few stalled attempts before they get there.

A person's ability to make positive changes will very much depend on their individual circumstances. Some illnesses (including mine) are fluctuating in nature, which means that one day can be vastly better or worse than the next, and for some people, the impact of their illness and symptoms is sadly so severe that they won't be able to do very much to improve their quality of life at all. Lastly, I hold a deep hope that perhaps a medical professional or two will decide to pick this book up and see its benefits – if that's you, thank you for having an open mind to this.

Part One
Once upon a time... (my real-life story)

1

The (relative) calm before the storm

My story starts in my early teens. Up to then, I'd been a happy child: living life to the fullest, with plenty of nature and fresh air around me, and lots of friends to have adventures with.

I'm not sure exactly when things changed, but I think I was around thirteen years old when I started experiencing general pain and discomfort that made it difficult to sit at ease, as well as almost constant severe PMS-like symptoms. After a couple of years, I went to see my GP (doctor) about my 'women's health' issues. I was prescribed the pill in the hope of it providing some relief, but the synthetic hormones didn't seem to agree with me, making my PMS-like symptoms worse, not better. That medication also seemed to aggravate the other strange symptoms I was experiencing, so I knew I needed to come off it.

Around the same time, I developed issues with my concentration, especially with reading and listening/taking in the spoken word, and some aspects of problem-solving (maths, in particular), which impacted on my ability to learn and perform well in class. This in turn led to me struggling – and losing interest – in school. I had always shown real promise academically, and I particularly enjoyed learning French; but suddenly I was struggling to take in English, never mind a foreign language. I was only understanding fragments of what anyone was saying to me in my language classes, and this meant that I also had difficulty talking back to them (cue a set of poor grades for my French listening and speaking exams). It was a similar story with maths too.

These symptoms were having a detrimental impact on my life, but they were also problematic in the sense that I couldn't actually pinpoint what was going on. I didn't even tell my parents because I was embarrassed by what I was experiencing and I didn't want my freedom to be curtailed (I know it doesn't really make sense, but I was a teenager.). I just wanted to be out enjoying life with my friends.

However, as my symptoms became more intrusive, they also became more difficult to hide. After a disappointing set of exam results in fifth year of high school, I managed to improve my grades in sixth year, but I still only just scraped through Sixth Year Studies French. I then went on to university to study languages and business, and to this day, I still can't understand why I made that choice. I had managed to pass all my language exams at school, but not well, and my French teacher said that I'd never be good enough for a career that involved foreign languages. I guess I wanted to be fluent that badly; I was also probably hoping that my health issues would eventually be resolved.

At the end of my first year at university, I got a summer job with a clothing and homeware retailer, but I struggled with the temperature of the upstairs shop floor, which was well above 30C every day. I found this to be a very challenging physical environment: in addition to the chronic symptoms I was already experiencing, I developed fatigue, breathlessness and irritability. This came to a head when I collapsed and started shaking violently one evening after work. My GP was unsure what was going on, so when these episodes recurred over the following days, I was admitted to hospital. However, the hospital doctors were also unable to figure out what was going on. They suggested signs of heat exhaustion, but my core body temperature wasn't high enough to confirm that diagnosis. So, after a couple of days on a ward, during which the episodes gradually settled, I was discharged with the suggestion that it had been a freak virus.

After the holidays, I went back to university and resumed my studies, but throughout my degree I continued to experience the same ambiguous symptoms that had plagued me through school, as well as further 'health-related incidents' – all without any real answers. I won't go into detail, but one thing I did discover was that I was extremely sensitive to caffeine. It would trigger the same violent shaking episodes I'd had during that summer after my first year at university.

I really did struggle with the languages part of my degree. The first year wasn't too bad, because it was like a repeat of learning I had already done, but after that it got really tough, because I still couldn't take in the spoken word. It was all garbled to me. Thankfully, however, I managed to keep up with the reading and writing side of my language studies, as well as my other subjects, and I figured out ways of working around my cognitive limitations. In other subjects, I found that if I wrote things down, I could concentrate and understand them better, so that became a key part of my learning and studying approach. It worked well, but it couldn't help me in the same way with languages. So, after a challenging period studying abroad in France, I admitted defeat and dropped the languages part of my degree in my fourth year.

Unfortunately, by this point, my health issues were interfering so much in my life that I was finding it difficult to cope, and with the cumulative effect of some additional personal issues, I had what I'd probably describe as a bit of a breakdown. I call it my 'period of overwhelm'. This resulted in me needing some medical help and having to complete my fourth year over an additional year of study; but I got my degree in the end.

Though I had hit a low point in my life, I wasn't one to roll over and give in. I fought my way back from that difficult time (I'd say fairly quickly, actually), and though I was still experiencing a raft of troublesome symptoms, the list of which just seemed to keep growing, I came back mentally and emotionally stronger – and more equipped to live with my seemingly undiagnosable health issues. I did continue to try to seek help, but unfortunately, it was to no avail. I was passed from pillar to post by the medical professionals I saw and eventually accepted that I just wasn't going to get any answers. No one was looking at the bigger picture of what was going on with my health (they just zoned in on one thing at a time) and I'm actually pretty sure some of them had me labelled as a 'hysterical woman'. I can even provide evidence of this in relation to one specific encounter.

At one point in my late twenties, when I was experiencing what turned out to be a chronic bacterial sinus infection that was regularly flaring with acute symptoms, a rather patronising male GP told me I just had a cold and was a bit anxious. He sent me on my way with a prescription for diazepam. I was so disgusted by his treatment of me that the next time I went to see him I gave him it right back, unused. He wasn't the only one who treated me in this way, and I've often wondered if I would have received better care and been taken more seriously if I'd been a man. In the end, my sinus problems were eventually brought under control after two rounds of surgery, and to this day, I still have to manage this issue daily to avoid recurring infections (which I do get, but thankfully not as badly). Sadly, experiences like these really damaged my trust in doctors and medical professionals, and even now I'm reluctant to seek medical help because I don't believe I'll be given a fair hearing.

It may come as a surprise, but despite all this, my twenties were actually a happy time. After a faltering start, I'd learned to live with my health issues and focus on the positives in my life. I built a healthy social life, and I enjoyed swimming and long cycles along the canal bank nearby. I also joined a local netball team, and I even rediscovered my love of reading through women's fiction/romcoms (the kind I have now written myself). These light, easy reads were all my struggling brain could cope with, and I was so grateful for their existence – because they made reading accessible to me. I also got the qualifications I needed and started building a career in Human Resources (HR).

It's actually a time in my life that I look back on fondly, not least because during my third decade on this planet, things got a whole lot harder.

2

Not the most wonderful time of the year

It was in the second half of 2013, when I was in my early(ish) thirties, that the fun really started. And when I say 'fun', I mean 'hell'.

On top of my existing chronic symptoms, in July and September of that year I had two similar – and very odd – experiences. In the space of around two hours, I went from feeling more or less fine, to severely fatigued, breathless and foggy-headed, to the point that I was unable to think straight. By the time I was on my way home from work to my sick bed, I was staggering like I was drunk and was holding onto lampposts or whatever was in easy reach to stop myself from collapsing.

Both times, I developed mild respiratory symptoms, so I assumed that these were infections of some sort. However, I was baffled at how similar the experiences were and at how unwell I'd become in such a short space of time. On each occasion, it took about two weeks of rest to get back on my feet, but I wasn't quite right.

A few days before Christmas, I woke up feeling under the weather. I had been out with a friend the evening before, but it hadn't been a big one – just a meal with a couple of drinks – so I knew it wasn't a hangover. With my Christmas shopping still to finish, I just did what I'd learned to do over the years – I soldiered on to make sure I was ready for Christmas Day. But by the time I got home from the shops, I felt so weak I had to lie down.

When I woke up a while later, I could tell that something was wrong. I had developed mild respiratory symptoms and felt a bit feverish, and I was fatigued and breathless (as I had been previously that year) but this time it felt *much* worse. I also had a weird tremulous feeling inside me – like I'd been using a pneumatic drill and was still feeling the effects – and my left side (including my face) felt strangely numb. Then, when I tried to stand, my legs buckled, and as I exclaimed in a shock reaction, I discovered that my speech was affected too.

Luckily my phone was next to my bed, so I called my brother and (with noticeably faltering speech) asked him to come round. By the time he arrived, I had made it to my dining table with a glass of water, but I was visibly shaking, so he suggested I lie down on the couch. As he helped me up, my legs buckled again and my body burst into a violent episode of uncontrollable shaking and muscle spasms that catapulted me onto the floor. I found myself writhing around, fully conscious and aware of what was happening, but with no control over my body and crying out from the agony I was in. It was far worse than anything I had experienced in the past.

My brother called for an ambulance, but by the time the paramedics arrived, this episode had passed. It should have been a relief having the paramedics come to my aid – and I must clarify that I have the greatest respect for our emergency responders – but unfortunately I was regarded with what I can only describe as suspicion and scepticism. It was clear from the questions they were asking that they thought I had drunk too much and/or taken drugs the night before, and I wasn't telling the truth about it. This upset me and frustrated my brother.

Eventually, they took me into the Acute Receiving Unit (ACU) of the Edinburgh Western General hospital, but I was quickly discharged after the usual routine tests came back normal, with no explanation other than it was possibly a one-off viral infection (again). I seemed to have a lot of 'one-offs' in my life.

Back at home, I continued to have further acute episodes one after the other. By this time, my parents had 'joined the party', and at a loss, my brother called NHS24, who arranged for me to see an emergency GP at the hospital in case I needed antibiotics. To cut a long story short, I ended up back in the ACU for more tests, then was sent home yet again when nothing showed up. They could see what was happening to me, but they had no answers. However, the next day, the hospital called and prescribed antibiotics for a 'query urinary tract infection'.

Over the remaining couple of days before Christmas I began to feel much better, so on Christmas Eve my parents and I went to my brother and sister-in-law's house as planned. I was hoping for an enjoyable but low-key family celebration after my ordeal, but unfortunately I woke feeling unwell once again on Christmas

Day. Rather than letting everyone know this, I played down how I was feeling. We'd booked Christmas dinner at a local hotel, something our family seldom did, and it was a treat for my mum to have a year off from playing the role of 'head chef'. I most certainly didn't want to be the grinch who ruined Christmas, so I crossed my fingers and put on a brave face.

This turned out to be a big mistake when my body went into meltdown halfway through my starter, but the staff acted quickly and I was wheeled out of the huge (packed) function room into a hotel bedroom. There, I experienced an episode so violent and so extended that I was screaming for someone to stop it.

Once again, the paramedics came – this time witnessing the episode, which went on for nearly an hour – and I was carted off to hospital. Again, I was pressed to admit whether I'd taken drugs, which really frustrated me. While I understand that they have to ask those questions, I felt more like the suspect in an interrogation than a patient who was desperately unwell.

I spent Christmas night and the following two nights in hospital, where there was only a skeleton staff on duty. It was a very lonely, confusing and isolating three days at a time when most people were celebrating with family and friends. I can imagine it wasn't much fun for my family either. Thankfully, my symptoms gradually settled down again, and I was relieved to get home, but I still had no answers.

3

A life turned upside down

The beginning of 2014 was pretty uneventful, and although I was still experiencing a range of unpleasant symptoms such as mild to moderate fatigue, chronic pain and some sensory issues, I was able to get on with my life in a reasonably uninterrupted way. However, I felt torn over my career. As an ambitious person I was relieved that I was still performing well in my job, and I was getting great development opportunities, but I was aware that my health was becoming increasingly unpredictable. This left me deeply conflicted over whether to follow my career aspirations or listen to my body, pull back and try to address my health problems. In the end, with my need for self-fulfilment evidently stronger than my need for self-preservation – and having no reason to hope that I'd get answers or help from the NHS – my career won. I simply crossed my fingers once more that my health would hold up and kept going.

Probably unsurprisingly, it wasn't long before the cracks appeared in that strategy. In May of that year, I ended up in hospital again with a repeat of what happened at Christmas. This was when I finally got my first breakthrough. One of the medical team looking after me in the ACU had the idea to contact a neurologist, who after reviewing my medical history and present symptoms, said that she thought I had something called a Functional Movement Disorder. She explained that it was a motor disorder that came from the central nervous system not functioning as it should. It made some sense to me, but it didn't explain everything, as so many of my symptoms were not related to my motor functions.

I was placed on a waiting list to see a consultant who specialises in this type of disorder and was told it could be up to a six month wait. At the time, I wasn't too concerned, because the neurologist I had seen seemed confident that I didn't have a serious illness and my blood tests weren't showing anything concerning. Also, the acute episodes I had recently been experiencing seemed to be triggered only by infections.

Once again, I got back on my feet, but this time it was even more short-lived. At the end of June, I went on holiday to Majorca with my partner (now my husband) for a week. It was blissful and just the break I needed after everything that had been going on. However, on the last night, I had what I thought was a reaction to something I ate and I ended up in a lot of pain and discomfort. Again, I wasn't too concerned – I have a long history of food intolerances and skin and respiratory allergies – and I thought, with the right medication, my stomach would get back to normal after a few days, maybe a week at most. Sadly, that wasn't the case. Over the next three weeks, not only did my stomach not recover as expected, but all the weird and (un)wonderful symptoms I had experienced over the previous year made a comeback with renewed gusto. This included the episodes of uncontrollable shaking and muscle spasms. I was losing control of my body on a daily basis, which was not just horrifying but also agonisingly painful and exhausting. When this eventually happened in a very violent way at work, I had no choice but to take time off sick.

I went to my GP, who signed me off for two weeks to see if removing the pressure of work would settle things down again. For the first four or five days, my symptoms seemed to settle a bit and I was able to keep relatively active, so I was feeling hopeful about getting back to work quickly.

Then things really went downhill.

One morning – keen to continue my positive routine – I decided to go for a walk straight after breakfast, but on leaving my flat and starting along my regular route, I noticed that something wasn't right. My legs felt like lead, and it was taking all my effort to get my limbs to do what I wanted them to. The fatigue and breathlessness had also returned, and I felt shaky and sick. I forced myself to keep going for a bit, before admitting defeat and turning back.

Over the next couple of weeks, my hearing, eyesight and startle reflex all became acutely oversensitive, and my brain became foggy to the point that I couldn't concentrate at all (not even on the TV). I started to have problems with word finding and remembering names, and I developed problems with my speech. My stomach was also still causing me huge problems. It got to the stage where I could barely eat, because when I did, the pain and discomfort afterwards was unbearable and seemed to trigger these extended episodes of uncontrollable shaking and muscle spasms, which would leave me utterly depleted.

Despite all this, I was determined that I wasn't going to let whatever was going wrong in my body beat me. I tried to retain some level of normality, which included travelling to Northern Ireland with my hugely supportive family for my nephew's christening. Looking back, it probably wasn't the right decision to go, but I'm glad I didn't miss it. In fact, things reached a head on that trip when I collapsed and was attended to by an off-duty medical consultant, who advised my partner and family that I (and they) should not be left to cope with this situation alone while waiting to see a specialist. By that point, I was having multiple episodes every day, mainly after eating (even just small amounts), and I could barely walk ten steps at a time, but it was only a couple of weeks until my medical appointment and I was resistant to the idea of pushing things through. Eventually I had to give in, though. My partner and family were at a complete loss as to how to care for me. Much as I hated it, I had to admit to myself that I'd lost my independence and control of my body – something I'd always taken for granted would work the way I needed it to.

When my parents contacted the hospital, the specialists in the neurology ward were reluctant to admit me – they thought that seeing the other patients would make me worry that I was seriously ill and worsen my symptoms. However, after conversations with my desperate family, they agreed to admit me for a few days to run some tests and try to make me more comfortable.

The neurology ward was an eye opener. There were some desperately ill people there, making it a very sobering experience. While on the ward, as well as being seen by the neurology specialists, a gastroenterology consultant visited my bedside. I explained the issues I was having with my stomach, and they changed the medication the GP had given me to one they thought would be more effective. Within a day or so of taking this new prescription, I was able to digest food a bit more comfortably, and contrary to the predictions that being on the ward would make my symptoms worse, the uncontrollable shaking and muscle spasm episodes began to reduce in frequency and severity.

Quick sidebar – I've since discovered that the issue in my stomach is something called dysmotility, which means that the muscles in my digestive system aren't working as they should. This is why I've experienced such severe gastrointestinal issues, and I now depend on two different medications to be able to eat (and function!).

After three nights in hospital, I was discharged. I was still very unwell, but I was at least a bit more stable. Then around a week later, in mid-August, I saw the neurology specialist I had been referred to for the first time. He went through my medical history and did a thorough physical assessment. With intense fatigue, breathlessness from the slightest exertion, continuous pronounced bodily tremors (a new symptom) and further deteriorated speech, it was an exhausting experience, both physically and mentally. Once he had completed his assessment, the neurologist told me that, based on what he was seeing and hearing and the test results from my hospital stay showing no sign of neurological disease, he was able to confidently confirm the diagnosis of a functional disorder. However, it wasn't just a movement disorder. He said that the broad range of symptoms I was experiencing (including my severe gastrointestinal symptoms) meant that I have what's called Functional Neurological Disorder (FND). He explained this condition in a way that was easy to understand, and after twenty years of confusion and frustration, I finally had some answers – the main one being that I didn't have multiple different things wrong with me. The problem was with the part of me that controls almost everything my body does, so it just seemed that way. He also told me that I had done extremely well to get to where I was (with my academic qualifications and career) when I had been up against such a challenging health situation for so long.

Interestingly, at the time of my FND diagnosis, my test results showed an abnormality in another area, and after seeing an endocrinology consultant, I was also diagnosed with Hashimoto's Disease. This is an autoimmune condition whereby my body is producing antibodies that are attacking and destroying my thyroid gland, and again there is no cure. So, I guess I have a bit of a double whammy going on, which makes it difficult to know which condition is causing which of my symptoms. Because of this, I tend not to focus on what is what and just manage it as one situation. And because my FND causes such a wide range of symptoms, it is without doubt the bigger issue for me.

So, what exactly is FND? To cut through the jargon, having FND means that my central nervous system (which is essentially the body's control centre) isn't functioning properly, and there's a problem with the messaging between my brain and body. FND is not a degenerative disease, but there's no known 'cure', and as you've possibly picked up from my story so far, the symptoms can be as disabling as those of Multiple Sclerosis, Epilepsy and Parkinson's Disease. There are treatment options that seem to have some success. Some people do get better, which in a lot of cases just means their symptoms improve to a manageable level rather than going away enitrely, but sadly some don't recover and some lose their independence altogether.

An analogy that's used among neurologists who specialise in this disorder is that it can be likened to a computer software problem, meaning that there's nothing structurally wrong and it's more of a programming issue. But the frustrating thing for people with FND is that, when we 'crash', you can't just switch us off and switch us back on again.

The next obvious question is, why has this happened to me? No one can answer that in any certain terms, as FND is not yet properly understood and neuroscientists quite openly admit that there is still a lot we don't know about how the brain works. There has been limited research into the condition, despite it being one of the top reasons for neurology consultations, and FND Hope (a charity committed to improving awareness and campaigning for effective treatment pathways) calls it 'the most common disorder you have never heard of'. I suspect that the lack of progress with FND research relates to it being regarded similarly to other illnesses like Chronic Fatigue Syndrome (CFS/ME) and Fibromyalgia. Like those with CFS/ME and Fibromyalgia, people with FND have long been stigmatised and accused of malingering (i.e. making up their illness for their own gain) or it being 'all in their heads', when these are all very real illnesses that destroy lives.

In the case of FND, some of this unhelpful attitude stems from the fact that historically it has been classed as a psychological disorder (known as Conversion Disorder) where patients convert psychological distress into physical symptoms. While there are some patients who believe their FND has been triggered by a significant psychological event in their lives, there are many for whom this explanation makes absolutely no sense. I'm one of them. Because having lived with this condition for over thirty years, I know that I didn't experience anything of the sort. Nor did I have mental health issues as a child. Also, over the years, a clear pattern has emerged with my symptoms (including my episodes of uncontrollable shaking and muscle spasms) – they are often triggered or worsened by environmental or biological factors that challenge my body, such as infection and fever, extreme temperature changes (both hot and cold), motion, overexertion, lack of sleep, PMS and products containing caffeine or other stimulants. Maybe one day someone involved in FND research will read this and find it of interest.

Thankfully, as I have said above, I'm far from the only person with FND for whom the traditional 'conversion disorder' theory doesn't fit, and it's now widely accepted among FND specialists that a person doesn't need to be stressed, depressed and/or anxious to have it. I can of course get stressed sometimes, the same as anyone, but the main cause of stress in my life has been my illness and symptoms. Sadly, this message is taking too long to reach and/or be accepted by medical professionals more widely. Since being diagnosed, I've come across stories of others with FND who have had awful experiences, and I consider the treatment of these patients nothing short of despicable. Fortunately, however, there are some great medical professionals out there, who properly listen to their FND patients and treat them with the respect and compassion they deserve.

As someone with significant lived experience of this illness, I know that there's still a long way to go with the research and I can categorically state that the impact on the quality of life of debilitating FND symptoms is huge. If anyone who doesn't believe it's a real illness were to spend just one day in the body of someone experiencing those symptoms, I guarantee they would quickly change their mind.

4

Finding my way back

On the day my diagnosis was confirmed, I was sent away with a clear message: I would have to work hard to 're-train my brain', and if I didn't, I wouldn't get better.

While I hadn't yet fully digested and accepted my diagnosis (more on this later), the neurologist's explanation made sense and I knew that there were problems with how my body was functioning, so I took that message seriously and worked with the online self-help advice they had recommended. However, despite doing everything I was advised to do, it wasn't an easy road for me. Over the next few weeks, not only did my situation not improve, it deteriorated. Almost overnight, it was as if the programme in my brain for walking – which had served me so well for thirty-odd years – had been wiped and replaced with a stiff-legged, stooped, uncoordinated set of movements that were beyond exhausting. It would take me about four times as long as before to get from A to B, and my legs would also give way randomly. I spent a lot of time falling flat on my face, and I was covered in bruises. The good thing, though – and this was part of the advice I was given – was that once I'd fallen down a few times, I realised it wasn't that bad and that a few bruises are preferable to living the life of a hermit. I was however, at that point, fully dependent on others to accompany me anywhere I went.

On my second visit to see the specialist, he acknowledged that there had been a deterioration in my condition, so I was referred to a neuro-physiotherapist. While waiting for this support, I kept working with the self-help advice and tried to remain as active as I could by taking short walks, even though it was a gruelling and painful experience every time.

One morning, an ex-boss of mine visited and took me out for a coffee, and she asked me a question: as I was off work, with time on my hands, was I working on the book I'd always wanted to write? My initial reaction to this was one of incredulity. Being as unwell as I was – and especially being so challenged cognitively – there was no way I was fit to do such a thing. But later that day, her question began circling in my mind. All my rehabilitation to that point had been focused on the physical side of things, but I had nothing to get my cognitive functions working again. Maybe a personal project was just what I needed.

So – inspired by the genre that had reignited my passion for reading in my twenties – I started writing a humorous women's fiction novel. I spent short amounts of time at my computer (starting from about ten minutes per sitting because that was all I could cope with) and I built up from there. It was exactly what I needed. More amazingly, as I wrote, it unleashed a level of determination I never knew I had in me. I was going to finish this book, and even if I never sold a single copy, it would be one of the most important factors in my rehabilitation – I talk about this more later.

Not long after I started writing, I saw the neuro-physiotherapist for the first time, and she helped me re-learn how to walk properly. She was also able to help me with my visual and auditory issues. This was by far the most effective treatment I had, and by Christmas, I was much improved in these areas.

I was willing to try anything that could help me rehabilitate. In the months after my diagnosis, I had some neuro-psychotherapy sessions, I did a mindfulness programme, listened to relaxation CDs, and tried chiropractic, acupuncture and the FODMAP diet to see if that would help with my digestive issues, but none of these things made any significant difference. I also tried beta blockers and different types of anti-depressants, having been told that they can help some people with functional symptoms by calming the nervous system response, but I wasn't able to tolerate either of these medications.

These have not been the only medications I've had extreme reactions to either. There are some that my body just can't cope with (including 'the pill', which if you remember, I tried back in my teens) while there are others are that fine – but there doesn't appear to be any clear pattern as to why. It has been suggested that it could be something called 'nocebo', which is when you expect to have side effects and then they happen, but in my case, this just doesn't fit. I've taken medications I've thought would give me bad side effects and experienced none, and I've taken medications where I didn't expect any significant side effects and the side effects have been severe, making it impossible to continue with them. Also, as I previously mentioned, I have a long history of food intolerances and skin and respiratory allergies, so there just seems to be a sensitivity there for me.

Anyway, back to the main point of the story. That period in my life had more twists and turns than a Thorpe Park rollercoaster, but while I was still battling a raft of challenging symptoms, overall I was improving. So, with my thoroughly battered confidence in my body beginning to grow again – despite going through the mill with my then employer, which included being forced to attend a stage one formal absence/capability meeting (more on this later) – I started to think about a return to work.

In January 2015 I went back on a phased return, only to leave three weeks later with a severance package as a result of another departmental restructure. I was nervous about being out of permanent employment when I had a debilitating medical condition that could make it difficult to find my next job, but nothing good would have come from fighting for a position in the new structure, especially when there was every chance my body would let me down again. Also, by this point, my priorities had finally changed. Walking away quietly would allow me time out to fully focus on my rehabilitation – and my new-found passion for writing was going to be a key part of that.

A month after I left my job, I did something huge (for where I was at that time). My partner accompanied me to London, where I attended an event to learn more about creative writing and get some professional feedback on the book I had in progress. It was a mixed experience. Physically, I found it very challenging – my stamina was low and the sensory overload I experienced through being on flights, on the underground and in amongst crowds was utterly overwhelming. This experience left me with a big realisation: while I had improved dramatically, I was still miles away from where I wanted to be and how I had been before. However, mentally, it was one of the most interesting and inspiring experiences of my life. I learned so much in a day and received positive constructive feedback on some sample chapters from my book that I had submitted in advance.

After I got home, I immersed myself in re-writing huge chunks of my book, which further supported my cognitive rehabilitation, and I doubled down on the physical side of things to keep that moving in the right direction too. I also broadened out my cognitive focus and spent a year working on what I'll call 'personal projects' to help me grow my mental and professional stamina in a safe environment.

This included setting up an HR consultancy business. I thought that being my own boss would give me the flexibility I needed to be successful in a work setting and that managing my own time would be better than trying (and probably failing) to meet the obligation of fixed working hours. I was still challenged physically, and the experience of being taken through the first stages of the formal absence (capability) process was a memory was that was so unpleasant and humiliating, I didn't want to risk being back in the firing line with another employer (excuse the pun). This all made perfect sense in theory. However, after a strong start, this venture sadly died a death when reality hit home. With my health still poor and unpredictable, I simply didn't have the stamina required for putting myself out there, making new connections and networking, nor did I have the confidence that I'd be able to physically make it to client meetings/premises when required. Maybe I would have had a better chance at it if virtual meetings and events were as commonplace then as they are now, since the Coronavirus pandemic.

It wasn't time wasted, though. I learned a lot about 'the new me' from that experience and the other projects I undertook, one of which was gaining a professional accreditation in Emotional Intelligence. This came at exactly the right time for me to draw bucketloads from that learning experience personally as well as professionally (more on this later too!).

I came out of that period feeling positive and reasonably optimistic about the future. By then I had even secured a literary agent, who was submitting my book to publishers for consideration. But there was still a big grey cloud looming over me. I didn't know how to get back into the workplace.

I won't go into detail here about my return to work and how I've managed my health and life generally over the years since, because I cover these in the main sections of this book. The short version is that my recovery has long since plateaued, I've had to fight hard to maintain the gains I've made, and I've had plenty of setbacks along the way. I work part-time and I'm at roughly the same level I was at when I temporarily left the job market. Also, with my health limiting what I can do in the corporate world, I've carved out a secondary vocation as an author. This I manage on my own terms, without the pressure of set working hours, tight deadlines and (exhausting!) office politics. I write when I feel well enough, and I pare back when I don't. And the best part is, I did get that publishing deal. Not with my 'rehabilitation book', but with my second, and I've had more published since.

My personal story is unique, but sadly, stories of individuals battling life-altering illness are all too common. Hundreds of millions of people across the world have disabling health conditions, and my hope is that that some of those people will come across this book and find it helpful. With twenty years' experience of undiagnosed chronic health issues, and a further twelve (and counting) spent battling a debilitating diagnosed condition that won't loosen its grip on me, I've worked my way through various challenges to ensure that I am LIVING and not just existing. Some things I've worked out myself along the way, some of them came from the advice of medical and third sector professionals, and some of them have been bolstered by my professional background in HR and strong interest in personal development. I'd also love to be able to say that I've done all this alone, but I haven't. I've been fortunate enough to have an incredibly supportive family, and my husband is my absolute rock. He's played such an important role in everything I've achieved with my rehabilitation and personal goals.

In Part Two, *Me, myself and I*, and Part Three, *Dealing with the outside world*, I talk about my experiences under different topics. These are areas of focus that I believe are essential for making quality of life front and centre during long-term illness, and as I mentioned in the introduction, there are also questions for you to think about under each one. I hope you find this content useful.

Part Two

Me, myself and I

5

Holding the mirror up

How looking inwards at myself is key to living the best life I can

If there's one thing I've learned from my life experiences to date, it's that I play a huge part in my own destiny. I've always held that belief to some extent, but never did this become more relevant for me than when I became incapacitated by my illness. I came across a fork in the road (metaphorically speaking) and there were two options available to me: I could either roll my sleeves up and stride determinedly down path A, ready to battle anything and everything that got in my way, or I could shuffle hesitantly down path B, treating every obstacle as another thing that's out of my control and working against me.

To someone in good health, this choice might seem like a no-brainer. Of course you choose option A. But what a person who hasn't faced long-term illness can never properly understand is this: that fork in the road isn't a one-off. It re-appears continuously. Because deciding on your overall attitude to you own illness is one thing, but being faced with endless blockers, barriers and setbacks while just trying to go about your daily life, is quite another – especially on a bad day.

So many illnesses aren't linear. They're more akin to riding the waves in an ocean where it's impossible to predict if you're going to face a small swell or a mammoth looming crest that could take you under with it. There's also something about feeling so physically broken that it can become extraordinarily difficult to keep fighting on – especially when it can seem like everything is out of your control. Over and over, I've ridden those waves, and I'm still afloat, but I'm not going to gloss over the hard parts to try and make myself look like the messiah of chronic illness. I'm going to tell it how it is, and how I've done my best to cling to my board – all so that I can LIVE along the way.

Anyway, let's get back to dry land. I chose path A. I wasn't going to roll over and let this thing dictate my future, but I've definitely taken a wrong turn and stumbled onto tricky terrain here and there. This generally only happens on my most difficult days with my condition and not for long – and I actually don't think there's anything wrong with that. We humans are imperfect and we make mistakes. We're also not invincible and we all have a breaking point. Anyone who claims to be perfect and never take a wrong turn isn't being honest with themselves or others.

I believe wrong turns should be acknowledged, because they provide an opportunity to learn about ourselves and correct course. They can also remind us of what we want and why we want it. The thing to beware of is getting stuck in that bad place. For me, a way to avoid this is to keep holding the mirror up and looking at myself. Not in a vain or selfish way, but by asking myself, 'Why am I not OK? What's causing me to feel this way? What can I do to change this situation for the better?' Because one thing's for sure: most of the time no one else can do it for me. I also don't think it's a sensible move to put my health and happiness in the hands of others.

This section of the book (Part Two) focuses on my experiences of all of this – of looking in the mirror, seeing what's reflecting back at me and taking steps to improve my quality of life. It covers a range of topics in areas such as coming to terms with my illness, understanding myself and finding my new identity, dealing with shame and stigma, retaining a sense of independence and control, and managing the obstacles of day to day.

6

Why me?

Acknowledging the injustice in a healthy way

I'm not sure I've ever voiced this question verbatim – 'Why me?' – but I've had countless opportunities to ask it over the last thirty years, and I'll admit there have been moments where I've felt there's some injustice to having the health issues I have. However, at the same time, I'm well aware that life isn't fair and it isn't supposed to be. I'm not naïve. Nature is a wonderful thing but it's also cruel.

An occasional reaction or feeling that falls under the banner of 'Why me?' isn't self-indulgence, it's called 'having a moment'. We all have moments of annoyance, frustration, sadness, even despair – and when I say 'all', I mean people generally, not just people with long-term illnesses. It's part of life. Everyone has bad days, and it doesn't take a mathematician or a neuroscientist to work out that, if you're ill, you're probably going to have more bad days than someone who's not ill, and you're quite possibly going to feel them more deeply.

I know that when I was a teenager with hopes and dreams and little by way of life experience, all I wanted was to be like my peers and fit in. I didn't want my symptoms to hold me back and I definitely didn't want to be seen as 'different', so as I've already mentioned, my default setting was to pretend they didn't exist. 'If I don't admit that there's something wrong, then there won't be something wrong'. That was my mindset. Back then, I didn't ask 'Why me?', because I was in a state of denial, and at that point I could do that to a certain extent and get away with it.

I've wondered at times over the years what it's like to live life in a body that works the way it should. Would my life have turned out differently? Would I want it to? This is probably the part where I'm supposed to say that I wouldn't change a thing. Well, I'm sorry, but I would. I can't imagine there's a single person with chronic illness who wouldn't wish for it to be gone and not to have 'stolen' so much from them. That doesn't mean that I don't like the life I have now. I do – or at least, the parts of it that don't involve pain, fatigue, struggling with my body, etc. I can say that I have good things in my life, and perhaps even that I'm a better person because of my illness, while also wishing I didn't have it. They're not mutually exclusive concepts.

I often hear people say, 'everyone has something', but there's a big difference between someone who has a problem with recurring athletes' foot or seasonal hay fever and a long-term condition like Multiple Sclerosis, Chronic Fatigue Syndrome or indeed FND. I'm very familiar with the type of person who's never had to deal with debilitating illness beyond a heavy cold. They all wear this same expression when I talk about how much my FND impacts me that tells me they have no idea how to relate. And it's often followed by a comment like, 'Have you tried mindfulness?'. I call it well-intended ignorance. Anyway, I won't go into that now, as I'm straying into a whole different subject area that's covered in Part 3.

I suppose the point I'm trying to make here is that those people represent a life I myself don't know. What it's like to live your life largely free from health issues. It's a utopia that I haven't experienced, not for over thirty years certainly, and never in my adult life. I can't remember what it was like to have a body that just works the way it should. But what I do know is that, if I look at health on a sliding scale, running from those who never get so much as a sniffle to those with severe levels of disability and/or terminal illnesses, it's a keen reminder that I could be a lot worse off and I should be thankful for that. People at that furthest end of the scale have much more reason to be asking 'Why me?' than I do, so it's all relative.

When my body went into meltdown in 2014 and my life really was turned upside down, I was further along the scale I've just described than at any time in my life before that. It was confusing, frightening (at times), agonising and exhausting. At the very worst of it, I didn't even have had the energy to ask, 'Why me?'. I was operating on the most basic of survival instincts. I needed to eat but my digestive system couldn't cope with food. I needed to sleep but no amount of rest made things better. I needed to feel safe but I was continually losing control of my body in ways that were impossible to comprehend.

It was only after my stay on the neurology ward, once my stomach medication had been changed and my episodes reduced, that I would have been able to begin to process how I was feeling about things. However, my survival instincts must have been at play again (or denial had kicked in), because I was of the mindset that this had to be a temporary state and I was on a mission to get better. However, as time passed and my recovery slowed, realisation dawned that I was plateauing at my 'new normal'. That would have been a natural time to wonder why I'd been cursed with this illness. I certainly can't remember having such thoughts in any significant way, and I expect that, by that point, I was just so grateful not to be in the state I was previously in.

All that said, I've definitely 'had moments' over the years since. Occasions where I've felt a pang of injustice or a bit lost, and these normally coincide with a really bad day. When that happens, I allow myself to feel it and I don't beat myself up for it. As much as I've come to terms with my illness, in a way, I'm still grieving my old life, and I think that's OK. I also know that, while my feelings are valid, I don't need to put too much weight on them, because every moment passes and I know I'll feel differently in an hour or after a decent sleep. I'm not a wallower but I do allow myself a free pass to work through pent-up emotions every now and then. That to me is far healthier than hiding things away and living in denial in the way I did when I was young.

Food for thought...

- What feelings have you experienced about your illness?

- How do you cope with these feelings?

- If you're struggling to get past the question of 'Why me?' and any related feelings of injustice, what might help you move on?

If you're in the early stages of chronic illness (relative to me) or have recently received a diagnosis, you might be feeling a bit lost right now, just as I did at times. What works for each person is different, but some options for the third question above might include:

- Having counselling

- Sharing how you feel with someone you trust

- Talking and thinking about your illness less so that it doesn't define* you – and finding a more positive outlet to use your limited energy on

- Asking others to put less focus on your illness (where it's appropriate to do so)

- Shifting your own focus to what you can do rather than what you can't

These are just some examples of things that have worked for me and for others I know. Only you know what might work for you.

*by 'define', I mean take over your life to the point that you lose who you are as a person. I fully accept that it is important to acknowledge the impacts of your illness on your life (and I have done this with mine).

7

The path to acceptance

Coming to terms with my illness

The path to acceptance can be a tricky thing to navigate. Looking back, I'd say that I had two big areas of acceptance to reach with my FND: one was accepting my diagnosis, and the other was accepting that, despite my best efforts, my symptoms weren't going away, and I was dealing with a chronic illness situation.

With regard to accepting my diagnosis, I'll admit I struggled with it at first. But it wasn't a case of straight denial. I was accepting of the fact that, for whatever reason, my central nervous system wasn't working properly. I also accepted that there was a misfiring of the signals between my brain and my body and that my broad ranging symptoms were likely to have one underlying cause. Logic prevailed that I couldn't possibly have so many different things wrong with me, so I was happy to try out the self-help techniques that were recommended to me.

The reason I didn't immediately accept my diagnosis was because I felt like my accounts of what was happening to me were being moulded to fit with the 'positive indicators' for FND, and I wasn't displaying some of the key signs of that condition. FND is a difficult one to get your head around at the best of times, so with the pieces not falling into place as I felt they should, I did have some reservations. I just needed it to make sense, and it was these missing pieces, including the question of why this had happened to me in the first place, that left me with some doubt.

I sought a second opinion, which backed up the original diagnosis. Through that, and through further educating myself on FND, I was able to reach a place of acceptance. I think the thing that helped me most was finding out that others with FND have unanswered questions about the origin of their symptoms, the way in which they manifest and why they perpetuate (in that these factors don't seem to line up entirely with current thinking on FND). I realised that it wasn't just me and I read, through credible sources, that there's still a long way to go with the research into FND to fully understand it. What I took from this – and I know this is me filling in the blanks a bit myself here – was that where my situation doesn't fully fit with the current landscape of FND, it's perhaps because there's still much for researchers to learn about it as a condition. There's also the fact that I have other co-existing health conditions that could be skewing the picture slightly. All of this (what is known and what is unknown) was enough for me to be able to accept my diagnosis and move forward.

Having cleared that first hurdle, the second obstacle to acceptance emerged as my recovery slowed and it became clear that I was plateauing at my 'new normal', as I talked about in the last chapter. That was when I had the realisation that I probably wasn't going to get back to how I was before. It wasn't a light bulb moment. It was more of a gradual thing. For a while, I yo-yo'd back and forth between acknowledging that I might not get any better (not a pleasant thought by any means) and pushing to try and squeeze that little bit more out of my rehabilitation. I honestly can't count how many times I did myself in because I was frustrated and unwilling to give in. My body simply couldn't take the additional demand that I was putting on it, even when I went gently and incrementally about it.

It was actually on recognising that I'd fallen into this unhelpful pattern that I found myself thinking about my 'professional toolkit' for the first time. I had spent years leading and working on change projects at work, and now I was going through my very own personal transition – and a big one at that. So, I dusted off my textbooks (actually, that's rubbish, I used Google like everyone else!) and I grounded myself by looking at the various theories of change and transition through the lens of what was happening with my health.

This was powerful because it was a reminder that what I was experiencing was normal and in line with the very natural and human response to change. It also made me realise that I wasn't just experiencing one big change. With my health situation being so complex, fluctuating and drawn out, I had already experienced (and was continuing to experience) multiple change events and the associated emotional responses that go with them. But whether I was on my third change event or my thirteenth, at that specific point something became obvious to me:

I was starting to feel like a pinball in a pinball machine in relation to my stalled recovery. I was bouncing back and forth between a rock and a hard place – and I needed to find a way to move on.

Once I had this realisation, it should have been reasonably straightforward to move on, right? Wrong. Accepting that I had an illness I'd been told I could theoretically recover from, was not easy. I'd have to acknowledge that I had reached the limits of my rehabilitation and this made me feel like I'd failed or I hadn't tried hard enough. It wasn't a nice situation to be in because I felt like it was my fault – and I had tried damn hard! Why couldn't I do it when others have apparently been able to? I had also received mixed messages about how to get better. On one hand, I was told I would have to work very hard to recover, but on the other, I was being told not to focus on my symptoms and get on with life as best I could. I mean, being able to just 'ignore my way out of my illness' would have been awesome. But that had never worked for me in the past, so I don't know why I thought things might be different this time round, when I was more unwell than I'd ever been.

With all of the above in the mix, it's no wonder I was struggling to reach a place of acceptance. And that was before adding in the unhelpful comments and the sceptical and/or baffled looks from people who didn't understand what I was going through, and who didn't have the first clue how it felt to be in my body. There was undoubtedly a feeling of shame in there adding to my reluctance to give in and accept that this illness was going to be a long-term situation. I actually remember saying to my neurologist one day in frustration, 'It's just the most ridiculous thing to have wrong with you'. This was obviously embarrassment... shame... the feeling of the stigma associated with FND bearing down on me. This is a subject I cover in more depth in Chapter 27, *Shame on you*.

In the end, for me – and probably for many people – reaching acceptance wasn't about giving in to my illness and letting it define me. It was understanding that recovery in FND patients is often improvement, not complete eradication of symptoms, and acknowledging that my FND was not going to magically disappear anytime soon. It was accepting that I now had limitations (meaning my life would look different to before) and continuing to battle against my symptoms every day to maintain the level of recovery I had reached and avoid slipping backwards.

Because it *is* an ongoing battle – and it's no picnic. Part of my acceptance was also making peace with the embarrassing aspects (particularly when they happened in public), such as collapsing or losing control of my body, so that I could continue to have a life and not hide away in fear of something going wrong. I still feel people's eyes on me when I have an episode in public, but instead of being concerned about this, I now try to focus on myself and what I need in the moment to get through it and beyond.

I've long accepted my situation, but I'll never stop pursuing a reasonable quality of life. To me, that's something worth fighting for.

Food for thought...

- Where are you on the path to acceptance and what does that feel like? You may find this hard to answer in a general sense, so if it helps, look at where you are in relation to a certain aspect of your illness like I have.

- If you're struggling to reach a place of acceptance, what might help you get there? If you're stuck, you might find it helpful to look back at the suggestions in the *Food for thought* section in the last chapter.

8

The art of self-discovery

How understanding myself is one of my greatest strengths

Quite early on in my career I attended an influencing skills training course. It was a two-day workshop that, for the most part, focused on different influencing styles (how and when to use them), but there was also a section within that learning programme on personal values. It's so long ago now that I can't remember why it was included alongside the influencing content, but that's by the by. What's important is the impact that it had on me.

If you're not familiar with or clear about what I mean by personal values, I'm talking about the deeply ingrained beliefs and principles we hold that act as our compass in life – basically, what's important to us. They inform our thoughts, feelings, actions, and decisions.

During this part of the course, I and the other attendees were given a set of cards with different values on them and asked to select the ones that we identified most closely with. It doesn't sound like a life-changing moment, but for me it genuinely was, and it has shaped how I live ever since. Here's why...

When I had selected my values and they were staring back at me from the table, I realised something huge (with prompting from the trainer, I can't take all the credit). My ground-breaking moment was that I wasn't living my life in alignment with those values – the things that were most important to me.

This was a proper 'aha moment', and as someone who is very interested in (and open to) personal growth, it immediately had me questioning why this was and what it meant for me and my life. I wasn't an unhappy person – far from it – but I had been feeling 'unsettled' for a long time. I had never fully connected with my career choice and had always felt like something was missing, and suddenly the reason why was laid out in front of me.

Two of the values I had chosen were 'freedom' and 'creativity', and I was in a corporate career that afforded me little of either.

I'd like to say that from there, everything slotted into place, but that's not generally how life goes – and it wasn't how mine went. To get to the good stuff I had to unravel a bit, become even more unsettled, and for a period, just suck it up.

(As an aside, I did also learn other things from that personal values activity, but I've chosen just to share the most impactful one.)

Anyway, I wasn't going to be able to make any immediate changes to my life, but the seed had been planted, and I finally knew who I was in a way that I hadn't quite grasped until that point in my life. Luckily, I was a keen learner and I was ambitious, so as long as I had challenging projects with a smattering of creative opportunity to sink my teeth into, and I kept getting development opportunities (which I did), I could accept that I wasn't 'living my best life'.

I mean, who really does? How many of us get the opportunity to do the thing that completes us? How many of us figure out what that even is? And as I said, I wasn't unhappy. I still got a lot from my career. It was just that I had a thirst for something more... something truly creative.

In this book's introduction, one of the areas of personal development I talked about having a special interest in – both personally and professionally – is emotional intelligence. I've done a lot of self-development in this area and aligned many of my work projects with its principles, which I think are hugely valuable. Working on my own emotional intelligence has helped me immensely over the years since I first discovered its value, including during the time I was at my most vulnerable with my illness. I've learned a lot about myself – my areas of strength and my weaknesses, how to keep things in balance, and that there are differences in how I was before my illness and how I am now. I've also learned that I need to be kind to myself because it's harder to be all the things I want to be when I have physical symptoms that chip away at me every day.

I've dug deep for number of years now, and as a result, I have a strong sense of who I am and how I need to live to be at peace with myself. It's paid off well. It has helped me shape my life so that I'm content and not at odds with myself, and this has been particularly useful over the last ten plus years while dealing with the worst effects of my illness. Because let's face it, it's hard enough having ongoing health issues without experiencing inner turmoil over who we are and what we need/want from life at the same time (perhaps without even knowing that's an inner battle going on inside us).

That's not to say that I haven't experienced a bit of this from my FND creating havoc in my world (covered in the next chapter, *Who am I now?*). But having a good understanding of myself has made it easier for me to jump the hurdles as they've come up, and I don't think it's ever too late to start working on this. I'll share a couple of examples of how I've benefitted.

In the last chapter, I talked about my path to acceptance that I was in a long-term illness situation. In addition to accepting that I wasn't getting better anymore, I also had to break the cycle of trying do more than my body could cope with. This wasn't just about moving on mentally and emotionally; I was caught in a pattern of behaviour that I didn't know how to get out of or why I kept repeating the same mistake, over and over.

This was during the time when I was setting up my (now defunct) consultancy business, and while working on that, I came across one of my old emotional intelligence self-assessments. Intrigued, I dipped into it for a reminder of how I scored in the different areas, and I found the answer to the issue I was having. One thing I had learned about myself back then was that my need for self-fulfilment was exceptionally strong, to the point that it could be a hindrance as well as a strength. My drive to 'achieve stuff' was so overpowering that I was sometimes shooting myself in the foot in other respects, such as how I was being perceived by others (like my then manager).

I had worked hard to pare myself back and get things into relative balance and had been quite successful with this. However, with everything that had happened to me in 2014, I had taken my eye off the ball, and after a quieter period when I was too unwell to do anything, my (renegade) thirst for achievement was back – unchecked and creating chaos in my rehabilitation. Through this realisation came another: I had to face up to the fact that my body could no longer keep up with my ambition. It was a tough one to stomach, but I was finally able to reel myself in, deal with it emotionally and reset my boundaries – and I'm glad that I did.

Had I not reminded myself of that problem area, I could well have found myself in a never-ending spiral of self-destruction.

Another example of how understanding myself well has helped me with my illness relates to my writing career. As I talked about in my real-life story in Part One, I started writing to aid my cognitive rehabilitation, and it was invaluable for that. However, it also provided so much more. I could have given it up as soon as it had served its initial purpose, but I realised that, for the first time, I felt complete. Why? Because writing fiction aligned so well with the two core values I mentioned earlier: 'freedom' and 'creativity'. Through writing my first book, I wasn't just letting my previously constrained creative juices flow, I also felt free. I was building a whole new world on (virtual) paper and it was all mine. It also – very importantly – gave me back a sense of purpose at a time when I was lost.

Having a sense of purpose is widely regarded as a core human need. We want to feel useful, important, needed, like there's a point to our existence, and if we don't it can have a terrible impact on us psychologically. Writing made me feel like I could do something useful, and even better than that, it was an almost perfect fit with who I am. Discovering all this meant that I learned even more about myself and I treated it like the gift it was. Once I'd written my first book, I knew there would be more, and the best thing about it was that it was something I could do within the confines of my illness. It became a flexible add-on to working part-time.

One final thing that I think is important to add here is that I don't always love writing. There are plenty of days where I'm not feeling it or where my symptoms are bad and the temptation to do nothing is strong. I allow myself a pass from time to time, but not often, because I know my writing is helping to keep me well. I remind myself that falling down a slippery slope because my brain and body are protesting is not the way forward. I keep going – within the limits of what I can comfortably manage – because I know who I am and I know what I need (even if I don't always like it). I also know that living a life that's at odds with what's important to me, what gives me a sense of purpose and what makes me happy will take its toll over time. Now, more than ever, I can't afford to let that happen.

Food for thought...

I can't overestimate how much it has helped me to gain a better understanding of myself and make sure I'm living a life that feels in reasonable harmony with who I am. It has been especially important now that I don't have as much independence as I used to.

By answering the questions below, you can start to get a sense of how well you really know yourself, how closely your life aligns with what's important to you and then see if there are any changes you might be able to make to help you feel more at peace – even during long-term illness. This is quite a meaty task, so I'd suggest working through it gradually and then revisiting it a few times. You might also benefit from asking someone you trust to give you their thoughts too.

- What five words would you use to describe yourself?

- What gives you a sense of purpose in life?

- What are you good at?

- What are you not good at – and how can you feel OK about this?

- What matters to you most? Try coming up with five different things.

- How well does the way you live your life align with your answers to the above questions?

- If there's a gap, what could you do to help these areas better align?

9

Who am I now?

Building a new(ish) identity for myself

In the last chapter, I talked about how I previously put considerable time and energy into understanding myself and I shared how this has benefitted me. However, I also briefly mentioned that my efforts towards self-discovery were not unaffected by my FND creating havoc in my world. Now is the time to put some meat on the bones with respect to that statement.

Let's recapture the scene. I was reasonably content. I had things generally figured out. I knew what I wanted from life (if not how to get it), what was important to me and where my red lines were, and I was continuing to move things in the right direction. Then came 2014 and my world and everything I've learned about myself was shattered. All that I was used to – my routine, my sense of purpose, my social life – was wiped out. It was as if a huge bowling ball had ploughed its way through my life and the bugger who threw it had got a strike.

Months later, once I'd rehabilitated enough to think about anything more taxing than eating, sleeping and my recovery, I had to pick up the pieces and see what was left.

Spoiler alert: it wasn't pretty.

Aside from becoming undesirable as an employee, I think the part I felt the most deeply was the loss of my social life. With this happening in my early-to-mid thirties, it felt like there were two crowds – the 'new or new(ish) parents' and the 'we'll party 'til someone or something stops us' crowd – and when I reached the stage in my recovery where I was able to do a bit of limited socialising again, I realised that I didn't fit into either of them. In fact, I didn't fit anywhere, because there wasn't a crowd for people with lifestyle-limiting chronic illnesses (not in my social stratosphere, anyway).

It's a funny thing, trying to work out who you are when only part of you has changed and it's not been your choice. I mean, I was still me... wasn't I?

Well, I dug deep once more, and the good news is that I am still me. I still find enjoyment in most of the same things, and I haven't had a personality transplant. But having different and/or reduced abilities has created two big changes in relation to who I am and what's important to me: I now prioritise self-care much more than I did previously (saying 'no' can still make me feel a bit guilty, but I have great respect for my need to do it), and I see the world through a slightly different lens. What I mean by the latter is while many of the same things matter to me, I now have stronger morals in the sense of fairness and social justice, and my eyes have been opened wider to the 'equality lottery' that is life.

So much of our world is still set up for survival of the fittest and I don't believe that's right. There's actually a part of me that might want to take on a more formal role in this space and advocate for people with chronic conditions, but what I know about myself is that I tend to take on too much (that pesky over-ambitiousness) and that then harms my health further. So, I'm doing it in a quieter way – through my fiction writing and this book.

I've even reflected on my personality type as part of my quest to figure out who I am now and this has helped me. I'll bring this to life with a short anecdote.

I've sometimes struggled with the dynamics within friendship groups. I enjoy meeting people one-on-one and in small groups of three or four. In those settings, I'm bubbly, chatty and often the outgoing one. However, when I find myself in large, boisterous groups with extroverted people I don't know well, that side of me is nowhere to be seen. I become the quiet mouse and feel unable to join in. This puzzled me for years. Then I did a personality test and I discovered that, on the scale of 'strongly extroverted to strongly introverted', I was almost slap-bang in the middle. Suddenly, it all made sense. I'm basically a bit of both, which is why I behave so differently in those different social settings. In a small group, I'm comfortable being more extroverted. If I'm with quieter people, I'll happily bring the energy. But in a large group with more of a 'pack mentality', I'm no match for the big loud personalities. In fact, they'll have me looking longingly at the door. Basically, I enjoy and get a lot out of being around others (when it's the right 'others'), but I'm equally happy to spend a good chunk of my time by myself.

Knowing this about myself and having thought about it in the context of my wide-ranging and challenging symptoms (including my very limited stamina), I'm now clear about who I am in a social setting and who I am unwilling to be. Unless it's people I know well and with whom I'm comfortable, the 'big group' dynamic is now an absolute no-go for me, as are social events where I don't know most of the people there. I won't force myself to go along and grin and bear it anymore, no matter who's invited me or who's going to be there.

Re-discovering and re-building my identity has been about both who I am and how I do life. Over a decade on from the day my life turned upside down, I might be limited in what I can do, but I've built a way of life that reflects who I am now and that works for me, and as I've already mentioned, I believe that I've become a better person for it. In fact, I consider it something of a superpower that I have a better understanding of some of life's challenges. I have insight and the capacity to show empathy in ways that many people can't. Everything I've learned about my illness and how society views and treats people like me is now a part of who I am – meaning that I've probably shared a lot of my 'identity 2.0' on the pages of this very book. I'll never pretend that I've got it all sorted, because my FND throws new challenges at me all the time, but I'd say I'm doing a decent enough job of living life as the updated version of myself. And most importantly, I feel proud of who I am.

Food for thought...

- What impact has your long-term illness had on your identity?

- What does that mean for who you are and how you live your life now – and how do you feel about this?

- How can you make sure that you're living a life that's the best fit for you now?

If you're struggling with your identity on the back of becoming unwell, and if you haven't already, I'd recommend taking the time to work through the questions at the end of Chapter 8, *The art of self-discovery*. You could even answer them from the perspective of before your illness and after your diagnosis (or after becoming unwell if you don't yet have a confirmed diagnosis) to allow you to compare how and where things have changed for you.

10

Why did I do that?

Managing my thoughts, feelings, behaviours and actions

Let's start this chapter with a few quick-fire questions. Have you ever...

- Thought that you can't cope with your illness, then found the strength you need to keep going?

- Had a frustrated or angry outburst on a bad day then regretted it?

- Dissolved into tears then felt stupid afterwards?

- Felt like the world is against you, then realised you've overreacted?

If the answer to one or more of these questions is 'yes', then you can feel assured that having occasional moments like these is quite normal. The reason we experience them is because the part of our brain that deals with emotion is faster to act than the part of our brain that deals with logic, meaning our emotions can take over and trigger us to react before we've had a chance to come up with a rational (and calm) response.

Through their research on how the brain works, neuroscientists have discovered all this and more. I won't pretend to be an expert, but I do find it be a fascinating subject that ties in nicely with my other areas of professional and personal interest, such as emotional intelligence and the behavioural side of change.

One of the consequences of our emotional response being faster than our logical/rational response is that we aren't necessarily aware of the thoughts and feelings we're experiencing in every given moment, and this can lead us to act in ways that we don't feel proud of (as illustrated by the questions above). However, the good news is that we *can* learn to tune into our thoughts and feelings in a way that can help with our decisions, actions and reactions, even while managing a long-term condition.

So how has all this helped me?

Well, another thing I discovered when I went through my first emotional intelligence self-assessment nearly twenty years ago, was that I had lots of areas where I was strong, but I scored lower in impulse control. This wasn't a huge surprise to me. I tended to vent my frustration during challenging moments, and once I'd opened a chocolate bar, I found it hard to stop eating, despite promising myself I'd only have a couple of squares. It wasn't something that was out of control, but seeing it emerge as an anomaly in my results made me want to do something about it. Especially because, at times, I was experiencing regret over my emotional responses, decisions and actions.

I delved into this area further and quickly discovered that it would take some hard work, but I could learn to manage my thoughts, feelings and reactions better. I'd previously read a book about positive thinking, which had offered a simple technique to help with this (I talk about this in the next chapter) and using this, as well as the other development materials I had amassed, I worked hard to better tune into my inner dialogue and manage my 'in the moment' reactions. It took quite a bit of effort, but it did make a difference.

Then, a few years later, I discovered a book that was by far and away the best supportive reading I've come across in this area: *The Chimp Paradox* by Professor Steve Peters. If you haven't come across this (hugely successful) book, Peters presents a 'mind model' called The Chimp Model® that makes it easy to understand why we have these impulsive/reactive moments. It's essentially down to the very issue of the emotional thinking part of our brain (what he calls our Chimp) being more powerful than the logical/rational part (he has named this the Human). Reading his book not only helped me further, it made me feel better about having these blips – because I realised that I wasn't the exception, I was probably closer to the norm.

Gaining a better understanding of how my brain works in the simplest terms and learning to manage my sometimes-overactive Chimp using the advice in Professor Peters' book has been extremely useful, and it has given the logical part of my brain the opportunity to take the lead more often. Even simple actions like counting to five or taking a couple of deep breaths before I respond in a difficult situation can make a big difference, and these 'fixes' have become almost automatic for me now in many situations.

Of course I don't always get it right, and Peters actually talks about how it's very difficult (and in some cases impossible) to keep on top of your emotions or 'manage your chimp' when you're unwell. He also advises that health issues should be addressed before working on his techniques. I've found a lot of truth in his words, and I've identified a clear pattern of dips on the worst days with my health. Even though I'm in a long-term illness situation where I don't know if I'll ever recover (which means I can't fix my health first), I still think it's been helpful to apply his advice, and it has still been possible for me to make gains with his techniques. Even if I don't always get it right, I've developed enough of a personal skillset to keep myself on the straight and narrow when I'm struggling. I'm also able to recognise when I'm off par emotionally; just being able to identify my Chimp as the perpetrator in these situations makes a world of difference because I understand what's happening and I can forgive myself for any behavioural blips. At those points, I work harder to engage the logical part of my brain (my Human) and choose how to respond, especially when I'm interacting with others at work or in my personal life. I certainly don't need to make my life harder than it already is through unhealthy reactions and poor decisions where I can avoid these.

I'll pose one last question in this area: how often do you procrastinate and allow the noise in your brain to get in the way of you being productive and/or doing things you know you should do but don't want to? This is your Chimp at work again. And yes, it's powerful enough to hold us back from making progress in life. It's what's getting in the way when we give in to the urge to lie on the couch watching TV instead of doing something more productive.

Since my bodily meltdown in 2014, when my most debilitating symptoms became constant and eventually chronic, my urge to procrastinate has been stronger, which seems to tie in with what Professor Peters says about it being much harder (or even impossible) to manage our Chimp when we're unwell. It's not a big problem – I'm generally a motivated person, especially with work and writing – but when I'm battling with worse pain and fatigue or a foggier head than usual, the urge to lie on the couch and avoid tasks of any sort can be powerful.

Before, I would assume that I'm just not well enough to do anything and I'd let my Chimp win. That was... until I cottoned on to its antics. I realised that it can sometimes be hard to tell the difference between genuinely not being well enough to do anything and my Chimp suppressing the little bit of energy and motivation I do have for getting something useful done.

Now I use the rational 'Human' part of my brain to decide what I am or am not fit for, and I test the water physically before making that decision. Using this approach, alongside what has become a well-worn mantra for me – 'it ain't over 'til it's over' – I often surprise myself by managing to do more than I expected to, and that helps me feel like I'm winning (or treading water at the very least). But I do have to play close attention to how I'm doing to make sure I pick up on the signals that I'm running out of steam before I overdo things. One that's a major tell-tale for me is when I start to become crabby and irritable – which isn't much fun for my husband if we happen to cross paths at that point!

Food for thought...

- How aware are you of your thoughts and feelings and how and when they tend to shift? Think about physical signs, such as tensing up or changes to your breathing, as well as internal emotions.

- How well do you manage your thoughts and feelings and what impact does your illness have on your ability to do this?

- What impact do your thoughts and feelings have on your decisions and actions?

- What are your thoughts, feelings and reactions like on a particularly bad day with your illness?

- Based on your answers to the above questions, might this be an area you could potentially benefit from working on?

If the answer to the last question is 'yes', then here are some pointers for further reading to help you with this:

- No surprise – I highly recommend *The Chimp Paradox* by Professor Steve Peters. If, like me, you've exhausted all avenues to try and get better, it might be worth a shot. I know it's a lot harder to put his ideas into practice when you're unwell, but I've found it possible to make small improvements that can lead to a real difference. And if you've already read it, are you actively using the lessons from it to help you LIVE?

- If you're interested in the basics of how the brain works, I recommend a documentary series called *The Brain with David Eagleman*, or if you can't get hold of that, his book, *The Brain: The Story of You*, which the series was based on.

- If you'd like to learn more about emotional intelligence, you can go with a good solid read such as *Emotional Intelligence* by Daniel Goleman, the man who coined the term himself, or for an easy light-hearted introduction, you could try something like *The Little Book of Emotional Intelligence* by Andy Cope and Amy Bradley.

11

Keep your chin up

Supporting myself through my illness with positivity and self-compassion

There are loads of books and videos about positive thinking and they all tout the same potential benefits: happiness, success, improved confidence and better health and wellbeing. I don't refute any of this. I absolutely agree that a mind filled with bitterness and negativity is a destructive thing. It's like rot. You give it an inch and suddenly it's taking you over and making you sick on the inside. However, I also don't believe that having the right mindset cures all ills (or in this case, illnesses and diseases) or that we can 'think' ourselves better. That's very damaging rhetoric, which belongs in the bin, along with all sorts of other 'miracle cures', and I'd go so far as to say that anyone peddling that message is exploiting vulnerable people at their most desperate times in life. Obviously, this is just my personal opinion, but I know I'm far from alone in holding it.

So, what's my view on positive thinking? Quite simply, it's not the be all and end all, but it is a powerful 'tool' to use alongside others, and it has helped me improve my quality of life.

The first time I dabbled with the concept of positive thinking was during my 'period of overwhelm' in my early twenties. My dad gave me a book to read called *Beyond Negative Thinking; Reclaiming your life through optimism* by Joseph T Martorano M.D. and John P Kildhal P.H.D. It contained a simple process to help me tune into my thoughts and learn to manage them, which included replacing a negative thought with a positive one. I found this technique easy to follow and immensely useful, and I've used it countless times over the years since. It's quite an old book, granted, and there are plenty of newer ones and online resources along a similar vein, but it will continue to be my go-to technique because I know it works for me.

A lesson I learned back during that difficult period in my life was that, if I wasn't being kind to myself, then there was no way I'd benefit from the help and support offered to me by others. It would all bounce off me and be a waste of their time. Also, where's the logic in making my own life harder? I needed to be my own biggest supporter and show myself some compassion. It wasn't like I had set out to fail, made questionable decisions or acted in a way that was unacceptable or wrong. I was just being me and doing the best I could, and I had to find a way to be at peace with who I was – a big part of which included learning to live with the health issues I'd had since I was a teenager, which weren't going away. I worked hard at all that, until it wasn't just an idea, it became a reality.

While I did still battle with my health throughout my twenties, I do think the improvement in how I viewed it, myself and life generally really helped me create those fond memories that I look back on today. The optimistic outlook I adopted and my improved sense of self-worth led to me becoming a much stronger person, who (thanks to that and the other self-development I undertook) was able to cope a lot better when my health went really downhill.

Having an illness that wreaks havoc on my day-to-day life, trying to steal my confidence in my body and my joy, is the perfect fuel for negative and unhelpful thoughts. So is the idea that I might not get better and what that will mean for me, particularly as I age. And that's not to mention all the things I've missed out on in life from being robbed of my health. My brain has more than enough material to turn my life into a grim soap opera and keep it on repeat, so it's important that I put a lot of focus on the positives and what enjoyment I can get from life, and that I'm kind to myself.

I still wobble at times. I can't imagine there's a single person on this earth who doesn't, even if they don't admit it (including to themselves). But thankfully, when unhelpful thoughts and feelings show up, I have the tools to manage them.

Food for thought...

- What kind of thoughts do you generally have – positive and constructive or negative and unhelpful? You may need to spend some time actively listening to your inner voice to get a real sense of this.

- What positive and constructive thoughts could you replace the negative and unhelpful ones with?

- How might you remind yourself to listen in to your thoughts regularly so that you can build a more positive mindset?

- How do you view yourself?

- What can you do to be kinder to yourself and look after yourself, especially on a bad day?

12

Two feet on the ground

Staying grounded and maintaining a sense of perspective

The best place to start here is to explain what I mean by *staying grounded* – that is, keeping your focus on what's real and on the 'here and now'.

For me, there are two big factors that can get in the way of me staying grounded while living with chronic illness: one is that I have to rest a lot, which means I can have too much time to think, and the other is that I'm quite future-focused (I like to plan projects, trips, have things to look forward to, etc.).

When I had nothing in my life but my illness, I had all the time in the world to think, but with my brain and body resembling a crashed computer, my mind was uncharacteristically quiet. That was probably what you call a blessing in disguise. However, when I got my diagnosis and started my rehabilitation, my mind 'rebooted'.

My main concern at that point wasn't, 'Will I ever get better?'. I thought I could and would. The possibility of a full recovery had been dangled in front of me like a big juicy carrot.

What was front of mind for me was getting back to work and keeping my job. I remember one day I was trying to understand how long it would take to get well enough to go back to work, and in the eyes of the medical professional I was seeing, work should have been at the back of my mind. Because of this they labelled me as 'anxious' – they even openly admitted this – but they were wrong. I had very real and very genuine concerns, based on facts. I worked in HR, I had seen first-hand what happens to employees who are off for long spells due to illness. I had also already experienced a change in tone towards me from my manager (which meant I was talking about an issue very much in in the 'here and now') and I knew the clock was ticking.

Was I being irrational? Absolutely not. And I made sure I communicated that to this medical professional to set them straight (I'm not sure it worked, but at least I tried). I knew that it wouldn't be long before I was hauled through a demeaning formal process to address my growing absence record and assess my capability to continue in my job. The likelihood of that happening, based on everything at play at that time, was high. It was nothing more than a simple risk assessment.

And I was right. Not long after that, I received a letter inviting me to that demeaning stage one formal absence meeting – despite me communicating to my employer that I was making progress with my rehabilitation – and I knew all too well where that process could lead.

So, was I grounded when I asked that question about my job? Yes, I believe I was. I was drawing on my professional experience and relating it to the facts of my situation. The reality of the 'here and now' (at that point) was that my employer was already beginning to subtly apply the pressure. I had managed long-term absence cases myself, so I knew exactly what stage in the process I was at.

Staying grounded in the way that I'm talking about here in this chapter doesn't mean blocking out reality, it means seeing reality as it is and responding in a reasonable way. That was a challenging time for me and it was real. I wasn't making it up or exaggerating the possible outcome.

Now, let's look at an example of not being grounded. This only happens on those really bad days I've talked about, when I'm dealing with much more intense pain, fatigue and brain fog, and perhaps also having difficulty with my motor functions, including walking and just staying upright. Basically, when I'm at my most vulnerable and I'm essentially housebound. On those days, my future-focused mind can occasionally wander off into rocky terrain (path B, if you remember from Chapter 6, *Why me?*). It can start asking 'Is this me? Am I going to be like this for the rest of my life?' and 'How will I cope as I get older?'. (I'm in my mid-forties now, and I'm starting to become aware of my body ageing alongside my illness.)

Those are probably reasonable questions to some extent, but they're also big and scary with no easy answers (or no answers at all). And isn't it convenient that my brain only decides to ask them when I'm at my least capable of answering them rationally? That's the emotional part of my brain overriding the logical part again, as per the titbit of neuroscience I covered earlier in Chapter 10, *Why did I do that?*. My Chimp being at its most mischievous, as per Professor Peters' mind model.

I'm not grounded when my brain hands me these huge, loaded questions during my bad days and I allow them to take up space in my mind. And, of course, the resulting answers when my Chimp decides to fill in the blanks are unhelpful too and not based on facts. They write a story that's unlikely to play out in reality – meaning they're basically fiction (says the fiction writer).

Thankfully this doesn't happen often, and when it does, I can put the irrationality to bed quite quickly – even when I'm feeling lousy. How I do this? Well, with the example I've shared above, it's because the unhelpful thoughts only come with a specific set of circumstances. There's a clear pattern that I've identified and it's almost like a simple formula:

A bad day + too much time to think + a future focused mind
= runaway thoughts and not being grounded

My brain might not be at its best when I'm having one of my bad days, but thanks to the focused attention I pay to what's going on with me, I'm still capable of identifying when this 'formula' is at play and steering myself back onto path A.

Rather than succumbing to those unhelpful thoughts and feelings, I acknowledge them and address them in a way that doesn't allow them to mushroom. I tell myself, 'Tomorrow is a new day' (as in, things will probably look and feel different/better), 'These are just feelings, they're not facts' and 'This too shall pass' (a well-known and helpful expression about the temporary nature of the human condition). I even say them out loud to emphasise them. These 'soundbites' are incredibly helpful for grounding myself when I'm not in a great headspace. And the more I repeat them, the better they seem to work.

Wrapping up, I believe that staying grounded and seeing things as they really are is so important. I would even say it's one of the most important parts of keeping myself mentally well with my illness. My aim is to keep two feet firmly on the ground as much as possible – even when the path is littered with crap.

Food for thought...

- How good are you at 'staying grounded' – especially on days that are more challenging?

- When are you most likely to experience unhelpful thoughts and feelings and why do you think this is? You could even come up with your own formula that will help you recognise what to look out for.

- What might help bring you back to the facts and the 'here and now' when you're experiencing these unhelpful thoughts and feelings?

Some options for the third question above might include:

- Engaging in some helpful course-correcting self-talk as I've shared in this chapter

- Sorting the facts from the fiction

- Distracting yourself with a more positive thought

- Changing your physical environment

- Talking about your concerns with someone you trust

- Trying some breathing exercises or the 5-4-3-2-1 grounding exercise that you can easily find through a quick online search

13

(Not) tied up in knots

Minimising stress to aid my quality of life

Stress is one of life's killers. I mean that more in a figurative sense, but from a literal perspective, it's not necessarily that far off the mark. It's not a health condition in itself, and in short, sharp bursts it's useful. 'Healthy stress' keeps us safe from danger, and if things are working as they should be in our bodies, it generally only shows up when we need it most. 'Unhealthy stress', on the other hand, makes life much harder than it already is. If left unchecked, it can damage us physically and psychologically.

Stress becomes unhealthy when it sets up camp and becomes a permanent fixture. It's associated with a range of health problems and it's no surprise really. A constant state of overwhelm is going to take its toll on our minds and bodies. This is why, with a chronic health condition, it's more important than ever to manage stress levels.

When I saw the neurologist for the first time (the one who diagnosed me), they advised me to minimise the amount of stress in my life. This made perfect sense, given what I'd learned about stress through my job and how unwell I was, but it was also a bit of a conundrum because at that time the only thing that was causing me any real stress was my symptoms. They were making life impossible for me and I just needed them to go away. But I heeded this solid advice and have done my best to live by it since – though the reality is that it's not always possible to do so, especially from a work perspective.

Over the decade and a bit since that appointment, my personal and professional commitments have fluctuated vastly, as have my symptoms and my stress levels. What I've learned from this 'scientific study of one' is that the neurologist was right. Stress doesn't help my symptoms. But also, *not* having any stress in my life doesn't make them go away or even markedly improve them. Another discovery

I've made is that I don't cope with stress as well as I used to. Not really a shock but interesting all the same.

In the main, I have/have had two main sources of stress in my life: my health issues and my work life, which is a combination of my HR 'day job' and my writing.

Now, before the eagle-eyed readers among you point out that elsewhere in this book I talk about my writing being a huge positive in my life, I'll clear up that apparent contradiction. The part of the writing process where I'm in my element, either lost in my creative world or working through a particularly demanding editing challenge, is the part that is positive and my secret weapon and all of that. The part that can be stressful is the 'business' side of things: marketing and self-promotion, seeking new contracts, the expectation to 'write to the market', and the inevitable negative reviews – the positive reviews always far outnumber the negative ones, but bad reviews are like little grenades that can be very destructive to self-confidence. None of that featured in my life until I became a published author, and I'll admit that it was a bit of a shock to the system at first. It's not like you get 'on the job' training (or therapy, for that matter!). You pretty much have to work a lot of it out yourself as you go, and it's a tough industry that can chip away at your confidence and self-esteem.

I've struggled at times and considered on a couple of occasions whether I should keep going because that 'business' side of things was sucking the joy out of what had become such a positive part of my life. But like I do with most things in life, I worked my way through it and learned to see things differently and protect myself so that I could still enjoy the benefits. Those adjustments to my writer's mindset have included taking some control and creative licence back, and while they're not going to make me rich or turn me into a bestseller, I know they're right for me and my health.

My day job has also created varying levels of stress for me over the years. It's par for the course in the corporate world, where cost cutting is never ending, as is asking employees to do more with less. There have been times when I've been in great form managing my projects and times when things have been more challenging and frustrating. What I have discovered though, is that my stress at work isn't solely related to my working environment (the culture, office politics, etc).

The ups and downs of my work life are also strongly linked to the fluctuations in my health. Over a lengthy period of reflection, which has included temporarily stepping away from my HR career and then returning to it, I have done the same as I did with my writing. I've adopted a completely different mindset. One that's focused on doing the best job I can but without getting 'emotionally involved' and while prioritising my health. And I'm sticking to it, which is fantastic progress.

Taking that time out has also given me more data for my 'scientific study of one', which (in my eyes) has rounded things off from a stress perspective. For the period that I was out of the corporate world, my stress levels were probably at the lowest I've experienced in a very long time. Did I see a major improvement in my FND and health in general? I did not. It remained just as troublesome as ever but without the added layer of stress making it worse.

What I've learned about stress is that it can creep up on me without me even realising at first. So, I pay attention to how I'm doing, and if I pick up on signs that things are getting on top of me, I ask myself: 'What's going on? Where's my stress? What's making my life difficult?'. I basically act as my own internal pressure barometer. And when I come up with the answer, I figure out what I need to do to change it.

Food for thought...

- Where is your stress coming from? What makes your life difficult?

- What impact does stress have on your health/illness?

- What small changes could you make to help reduce the stress in your life? This could be changes to your daily routine, your commitments, how you go about certain tasks (at work or at home) or your mindset. Big changes are often hard to make due to financial, family, work or study and other commitments, but if you can identify a few small things that you can do differently, it can add up to a helpful improvement in your stress levels.

If you're struggling to come up with ideas for the third question, for some inspiration, you could jump to Chapter 18, *Who's in the driver's seat?*, which focuses on control.

14

When the going gets tough

Coping with life's challenges and building resilience

In the last chapter, I shared my two main sources of stress: stress associated with my work life and stress that's linked to my health issues, and I'd like to delve into the latter a bit more as I explore the topic of resilience.

For me, from a health perspective, stress isn't just about the mental and emotional pressures of being unwell – for example, the financial impact of not being able to work full time or the impact of an employer being unhappy about my sickness absence. I also (like many others with ill health) can't endure much 'physical stress' (including exercise) due to my fatigue, pain and pain sensitivity. 'Sensory stress' from the likes of loud noises, crowded places and motion is a problem. And because of symptoms such as brain fog, headaches and cognitive problems, some tasks that require mental focus, such as those requiring a lot of physical co-ordination and some aspects of problem solving, also take their toll and can push me into a state of overwhelm. My thresholds in these areas are a lot lower than the average person's – and as I used to pass for the 'average person' (well, more so than I do now), I'll share an example.

I used to be a great cook. I could manage ingredients lists and co-ordinate complex methods to produce multiple courses that were timed perfectly. Now, I'm a disaster in the kitchen unless it's something I've made many times before. With new recipes, I continually lose focus, get muddled and forget what I'm doing. And if there are multiple steps that I need to manage simultaneously, it's almost guaranteed that something will burn and something else will end up on the floor.

Now, I know that being a bad cook isn't a universal sign of a health issue. That's not the point of that example. The point is that the cognitive effects of my FND cause me to struggle with (and become overwhelmed by) tasks that a healthy person would be able to navigate their way through quite easily. It's also just one example of many. With so many sources of potential stress coming from my symptoms alone, when external influences come into the mix and rock the boat further, it can come down to an 'in the moment' choice of sink or swim. I therefore need additional tools in my 'toolkit' to keep me moving forward positively and productively.

Keeping my stress levels down is one go-to approach (as I've already talked about), but as I don't have control over every aspect of my life, things are going to come left field and catch me off guard. Additional demands, challenges and setbacks (both expected and unexpected) are a fact of life, so being able to deal with them while not allowing them to throw me massively off course is essential – especially because my energy is so limited. I need to use it wisely. That's where personal resilience comes in.

Personal resilience has become a big area of focus in workplaces during my career. It's basically the ability to deal with and recover quickly from life's problems and challenges. It's also sometimes referred to as 'bouncebackability', because it's about a person's ability to 'bounce back' from whatever setback they've encountered. The idea is, if you build your resilience, then you'll be more equipped to deal with the harsh realities of life.

I buy into resilience as a concept. There's a general theme of personal resilience that runs through the entirety of this book. The questions at the end of each chapter aren't just designed to help you have a better quality of life, they're there to help you take control of your life and improve your resilience – what I like to call 'building up my coat of armour'.

As I mentioned when sharing a bit about my symptoms in the introduction, the dysfunction I experience in my central nervous system includes sensory issues and overactive reflexes. The effects of this play out in response to sudden visual stimuli, loud noises and motion/vibrations (rollercoasters are absolutely off limits for me! Actually, so are the kiddie rides...), and they can also come through in how I react to issues and problems that come up in my life. In fact, my reflexes can be so fast that I once caught some items I had clumsily knocked off a shelf in a supermarket with such speed and deftness that the man next to me blinked at me like I was a superhuman character in a Marvel movie. I'm not even exaggerating!

Anyway, what I'm getting at is: with my physiological response to shock being so wonky, I can have an equally rapid reaction when faced with a sudden problem or setback if I don't catch myself first (and it's not always a helpful one like I experienced in the supermarket). I may not be the ultimate expert when it comes to 'in the moment' reactions, but thankfully, when I do have those moments, I also have the self-awareness to quickly see what's happening, course correct and move on – if I want to. In fact, sometimes I'm well aware that I'm having a reaction to something, and I intentionally allow this to play out, because it's better to get it out of my system than bottle up unhealthy frustration (though I'm careful not to impact negatively on others as I do). Or if something has really peed me off and I need to get it out of my system, then I give myself permission to vent to someone I trust about it, because I know it'll help. (Professor Peters actually encourages this as a mind management technique in his book, which he calls 'exercising your chimp'.)

I have a strong moral compass, which means that I can feel things deeply, but thankfully I'm also pretty good at bouncing back and getting on with things after a setback. This action of 'moving on' is a huge part of resilience, and I think being quite a future focused person probably helps with this. I might not forget (especially where I consider an injustice to have taken place), but I'm not someone who could wallow unproductively for long, even if I tried, because my natural tendency is toward progress, completing tasks and achieving goals. That's what gets me up in the morning and it's what makes me tick.

While it's important to build resilience – and I think it's great that it has become a big subject in relation to self-development – my personal opinion is that, as a concept, it can be misused and I have a bug bear about this. What I'm referring to is where a perceived lack of resilience is used as a weapon in blaming people for not being able to cope – and I'm not just referring to my twenty(ish) years' experience in HR, I've seen this play out across society generally. As in, if you can't deal with life's problems then you're not resilient enough and that's your fault. I consider that to be very damaging, particularly when it's aimed at people who are unwell, whether physically, mentally or both. The saying 'you have nothing if you don't have your health' has a lot of truth to it. And it includes not having as much resilience.

No one should ever be guilted or chastised for not having enough resilience, especially with the highly uncertain and difficult world we're currently living in. And they should certainly never be blamed for not being able to cope when there is too much expected of them or where they are being treated unfairly. They should be supported and shown compassion, while also being encouraged to help themselves. If humans really are the superior species we claim to be, then surely we should have moved beyond 'survival of the fittest' (though, sadly, that's not the case, as I've already mentioned in the introduction to this book). It's archaic and it'll never lead to a prosperous society long-term – well, that's my humble view, anyway.

A few times in my life, I've been told I need to 'toughen up'. I find this to be an offensive and ignorant statement, because it suggests that I'm not good or strong enough just because I don't always have a steely exterior. It's also ridiculous because that judgement is based on a person seeing me during a single moment in time, most likely where I haven't managed to stop the emotional part of my brain having a reaction. They don't see the part where I quickly move on with determination, or how I push through a debilitating illness every day so that I can have a reasonable quality of life. That is resilience, in a nutshell.

Food for thought...

- How do you react to obstacles and challenges in your life?

- What moments of resilience have you had during your illness that you can be proud of?

- What could you do to build your resilience further?

To offer a little inspiration for the third question above, ways in which you could build your resilience include:

- When something bad or upsetting happens, asking yourself 'Will this matter in...3 days, 3 weeks, 3 months?'

- Trying the options for staying grounded in Chapter 12, *Two Feet on The Ground*

- Reading *The Chimp Paradox* by Professor Steve Peters

Remember that resilience is a general theme that runs through this book, so any work you do on the *Food for thought* questions is likely to support you to become more resilient overall.

15

Vulnerability: the dark side

Exploring feelings of insecurity

If you look up the word 'vulnerability' online, you'll find a range of search results: dictionary definitions, government information, websites that cover areas such a disaster relief and computer security – they all point to the negative. They generally describe vulnerability as a state or condition of weakness in a person, system or process that's open to harm of some kind. However, in amongst those search results, you'll also find references to vulnerability as a positive thing in the context of opening yourself up – sharing your thoughts, emotions, how you're feeling – so that others can get some understanding of what's going on for you.

Both of these opposing definitions have featured in my experience of long-term illness, so I felt it important to cover them. I've chosen to call them the 'dark' and 'light' side of vulnerability, and as this is quite a meaty topic, I've split it into two chapters, starting with the dark side.

The dark side of vulnerability is real, it's painful and it can be hugely damaging. When I was at my most unwell, I felt extremely vulnerable in the negative sense of the word. I've already mentioned that, for a few months, I was unable to leave home without someone accompanying me. I had close to zero physical stamina. My senses (sight, hearing, startle response) were so messed up that I couldn't trust my brain to judge that there were no cars coming when I wanted to cross the road, and whenever a heavy goods vehicle would come rumbling past – which was often where I lived – my legs would give way and I'd drop like a stone. I could barely walk ten feet without coming to grief. All this made me feel vulnerable, and I'm sure I'm by no means the only person with a long-term health condition and/or disability who has felt this way.

As I rehabilitated physically and was able to do more alone, my first (and natural) instinct was to never put myself in a situation where I'd feel unsafe.

That was both the right and the wrong thing to do. We should, of course, never knowingly put ourselves in danger, and I didn't. For me, feeling unsafe was also knowing that my body could fail me at any given moment. I could fall or collapse or have one of my episodes while I was out and find myself stuck, unable to get home.

But if I wanted my life back, I had to introduce an element of risk into it. At first, I stayed close to home, and if I got into difficulties my partner (now my husband) would come and get me. Then, as things improved, I was able to take a bus into town alone – that was a *big* step for me. And things did go wrong. I did fall down. My body did go into meltdown at the most inopportune moments. But there were also times when it didn't, and over time that helped my confidence grow and my sense of vulnerability shrink.

Then there was the emotional side of things. My emotional vulnerability came from being unable to fend for myself. When things got really bad with my health, I'd been with my partner for a couple of months shy of two years, and we'd taken the decision to move in together just a few months before. In fact, it was the very week that I was due to give up my rented flat and move in with him that I found myself being admitted to hospital (and no, it wasn't a devious ploy to get out of the heavy lifting, for the cynics among you who are wondering). During that time, and in the period after, I found myself wondering if my partner would stick around. He hadn't signed up for this, and as much I was hopeful that I would get better, we had no way of knowing how well I would or wouldn't recover.

This feeling of vulnerability was probably in part due to the fact that my health issues had been brought up close to the end of a previous relationship I was in, even though they were minuscule in comparison. It had become clear to me back then that my ex-partner found them to be an inconvenience to his life (which they possibly were) and that this was part of why he was having doubts about us.

So when I got *really* sick, I became concerned that my current partner might feel the same (and more justifiably so). Thankfully he wasn't the kind to do a bunk at the first sign of trouble, and he became – and still is – my rock. However, even with that relationship stability, I still felt vulnerable, because I was (quite justifiably) concerned about keeping my job and being able to bring in an income. I've already shared in Chapter 12, *Two feet on the ground*, how I found myself on the wrong side of the formal absence process with my ex-employer. I knew that if I were unable to sustain my return to work or I had further periods of short-term absence, I was at risk of being dismissed. The idea of being out of work with a long-term illness was daunting, but I simply couldn't have the pressure of that formal absence process continuing to hang over me, especially not when I'd come so far in my recovery. Sad as it sounds, I knew that I'd feel less vulnerable walking away and being jobless and the redundancy package at least provided some financial respite in the short term.

When I did eventually find a job and get back into the workplace, everything fell into place and my feelings of vulnerability disappeared, allowing me to live happily ever after. No, of course they didn't. We all know fairytales that far-fetched exist only in our minds. The reality was that I still felt vulnerable. Each time I was off sick – which to be fair wasn't that often, given what I was up against – I felt a rumble of insecurity. Because, despite meeting with occupational health and having elevated absence triggers put in place, there were still uncomfortable conversations. Thankfully, though, I had enough support to carry me through, and I worked hard to show my worth. That's one of the unfortunate by-products of having a long-term illness in the workplace – the feeling that you have to work harder than anyone else to prove yourself. And I know I'm far from alone in feeling that way.

I could probably write a lot more about the dark side of vulnerability, but I'll stop there. The point here is: if you have a debilitating long-term condition, it's likely you've come up against this ominous force, whether you've consciously recognised it or not. And it's my strong opinion that feeling vulnerable and having genuine, well-founded concerns during chronic illness doesn't mean you're overly anxious. It means you're human.

Remember the chapter earlier on getting to know yourself and understanding what's going on for you (Chapter 8, The art of self-discovery)? What I had on my side at the most difficult times with my illness was that I knew myself well, and I knew exactly what was causing me to feel vulnerable. With that self-awareness came the ability to face my challenges and address them through logic and reason, instead of allowing them to take over me in unhealthy ways that could have led me down another path entirely.

Food for thought...

You can feel vulnerable in any angle of your life, whether it relates to physical issues, relationship issues, finances, family life, work or study.

- What aspects of having a long-term illness make you feel insecure and vulnerable?

- What small changes could you make in your life to help you feel a bit more at ease? These might include sharing your concerns with someone you trust, seeking support (including financial support), noting down what's bothering you and why to help you understand it or even taking baby steps towards facing your fears. Again, these are just examples, only you know what might work for you.

16

Vulnerability: the bright side

Being open and sharing in the right circumstances

Having explored the *dark* side of vulnerability in the last chapter, let's now look at the other side of the coin – the *bright* side. This is the idea that vulnerability can be seen as a positive thing: that if we're open and we share our personal situations and challenges, then others can get some understanding of what's going on for us and (hopefully) be supportive. If you want to learn more on this subject generally, Brené Brown, an academic who studies human connection, has a great video called 'The Power of Vulnerability', which you can find on YouTube. What I'm going to talk about in this chapter is how and why I've chosen to be vulnerable in the context of my long-term illness.

Through my experience of being unwell, I've often faced the dilemma of how much to share and who to trust. On one hand it can be helpful to share, so that others understand how things are for you and can have your back, but the more you share, the more you might feel in a place of weakness in the sense of feeling/being judged or treated unfairly (there it is, that pesky dark side again).

I've always been quite an open person; someone who tends to lay it all out there, and who can then sometimes feel a tinge of regret when I've overshared. Historically I've also trusted too much and been burned for doing so. With these feelings and consequences, you might wonder why it's ever good to be open and share. But taking a balanced view of things, I'd say that embracing the bright side of vulnerability – that is, being open, sharing, putting myself out there – has paid off more times than it has bitten me in the backside. And quite frankly, if someone is going to be vindictive, they can easily draw their own conclusions and/or make something up about me which will surely be worse than the truth in terms of impact. In a spun story, I can quickly be painted as the bad one, whilst if the real me is there for all to see, I'm simply trying to do the best I can in the challenging circumstances I'm facing. I might not always get things right, but then who does?

If I had chosen not to be vulnerable, I wouldn't have received so much support from the great people who have provided it, my quality of life might not be at the level it is now, and I wouldn't have had some of the positive experiences I've had.

The one that's most front of mind for me is my novel, *Take A Moment*, the story of which was inspired by my own health challenges. In this book, the main character, Alex, receives a shock diagnosis of Multiple Sclerosis (MS). This is not the condition I have, but there are overlaps in symptoms – basically, I didn't want it to feel too close to home and have the people who know me seeing me as the main character. Keeping things brief, Alex suddenly faces a new reality and an uncertain future, and on finding herself treated differently by those around her (not in a good way), she takes control of her own destiny and finds positive new relationships along the way. Vulnerability is actually a theme that runs through that story.

At the back of that book, I briefly shared my personal story and how my own experiences inspired me to write it. I made a considered choice to be vulnerable in doing that, and what did I get in return? Not judgement or nastiness, but readers with chronic illnesses sending me messages of gratitude and support; telling me how much the story had touched and inspired them and how good it was to see a person like them reflected on the pages. Or they posted on social media about the book in a similar way. Had I chosen to play it safe and not put myself out there, I would have missed out on all that positivity and on making that small difference to my readers' lives.

Choosing to be vulnerable can be hugely powerful and rewarding, but it should be a conscious and considered decision. It has also paid off for me in my current day job, in that I've been able to get the flexibility and support I need on an individual level and even drive positive change in the organisation, but that's because the right ingredients were there for me to do that. Most notably, I have empathetic and supportive managers who understand the challenges I've faced (and continue to face) with my health and who believe in building an inclusive workplace. Had I been working in a toxic environment or had relationship difficulties with my managers, I wouldn't have chosen to put myself out there in the way that I did.

A person can choose to be vulnerable in any area of life, whether it relates to sharing and seeking support with family challenges or speaking to teachers or tutors about getting help in a learning setting. Perhaps even opening up to family and/or friends rather than putting on that brave face.

Ultimately, deciding what and how much to share is a very personal choice, and these days I always consider the landscape around me before doing so. Is there enough trust? Do I have strong enough relationships with those around me (my friends, manager, teammates, etc.) to feel like I have the right support and a genuine listening ear? Do I feel strong enough to deal with any negative outcomes that could come from choosing to be open? If the answer is 'no', then I will now prioritise protecting myself over sharing openly. But if the answer is 'yes', then I know there could be great benefits to help me LIVE.

Food for thought...

- How much do you share about your health with others in your home life, social life and at work or study (as applicable)? And how comfortable are you with this?

  - If you feel the right conditions exist to be more open with others, how can you do it in a way that helps you feel safe? Small and tentative steps may be key here.

Feeling a little out of our comfort zone can be a positive thing. It can help us move forward if we're stuck. However, please don't ever take risks that might compromise your mental and/or physical health and safety.

17

The world's (no longer) my oyster

Finding the right balance of independence and support from others

Throughout my life, I've encountered people who rely on a lot of support from others and people who want none at all (I'm talking generally here, not in the context of ill health). There's no right or wrong way of doing things, but I would expect that those who operate at the extremes experience more bumps along the way than those who are closer to the middle-ground. That is, living independently enough, while also being willing to ask for and accept help when it is useful to do so. But people will get by how they get by, and as long as their lives don't depend on it, how they choose to live in that respect doesn't matter that much.

Now, throw in the complication of a long-term illness, and suddenly things get trickier. This is particularly the case for someone who has been very independent and is suddenly relying on others for the most basic of things. That was exactly what happened to me. I was brought up to stand firmly on my own two feet. I got my first part-time job at the age of fourteen (on an hourly rate of £1.85 per hour – I'm showing my age here!) and my parents both worked full-time, so I was expected to contribute to the household tasks. I've always been an independent thinker, not one to follow the crowd, and generally I like to find my own way in life. (Perhaps that's part of the reason why I didn't tell anyone about my health issues for some time – there's the downside...)

In the period prior to 2014 I was self-sufficient. I had my own career and income, my own place and I was 'adulting' just fine. So to have my independence whipped away from me in the space of a few weeks was one hell of a shock. There's nothing like falling on your face every few steps to make you realise that you've shot from one end of the independence/dependence scale to the other.

At that time, the instincts of my loved ones were to try to catch me before I hit the ground, but they were advised not to by my neurologist. And they were also asked not to pick me up off the floor. It sounds cruel but the reasoning for this was to help me learn that falling down wasn't so bad and to discourage an emerging pattern of 'rescuer' behaviour that could stall my recovery. It was about getting me to fight back against my illness, and whether intentional or not, it also helped me retain some level of independence when I was in my most vulnerable state. When I got knocked down, I got up again – by myself.

As I mentioned in Chapter 6, *Why me?*, at that early stage I was so unwell that I didn't focus too much on what I'd lost (in this context, my independence). My focus was on trying to get better, so I was quite happy to let people support me while I rehabilitated – and especially as trying to do certain things myself was either excruciatingly painful and exhausting or beyond my reach altogether. But as the reality of my reduced independence gradually sank in, I realised that things I'd previously taken for granted were no longer an option for me – and there was no real sign of that changing. For example, other than fairly short journeys or outings, I can no longer travel alone because at some point I'll find myself in difficulties. Apart from a couple of 'historical' exceptions, one of which I talk about below, I only take longer journeys/trips away from home with my husband, who fully understands my limitations and needs, and only in ways that I can physically cope with. I suppose, looking at it from a positive perspective, at least I can still travel within those limited parameters, which helps me feel like I still have some level of freedom if not independence.

I'm clearly more adaptable than I've given myself credit for in the past. Or perhaps that's just the nature of the human condition – that we're able to mould ourselves in whatever way is needed for survival (in this case, 'survival' being the ability to deal mentally and emotionally with the significant change and disruption in my life). Whatever the reason, I guess I've just got used to how my life is now. And I'm thankful for the limited level of independence that I do still have. It doesn't stop me wishing I could do more than I can though. I still continually push the boundaries to try to grow my confidence in my body and see if I can tease out that little bit more freedom for myself (though not always with success).

A few years ago, I really wanted to go on holiday and my husband couldn't take the time away from work, so I asked a friend if she would be interested in going with me. I fully expected her to say no, but she said yes. Surprised but delighted, I shared everything she needed to know about my limitations, and thankfully she didn't run a mile, so we excitedly booked a beach holiday abroad.

For me, this was going way out of my comfort zone. I hadn't travelled anywhere without my husband since before 2014, and while it was an enjoyable break, I learned that travelling with anyone other than him is probably a step too far for me. This was nothing to do with my friend – she did her absolute best to understand and accommodate my situation and we had been away together in the past (very successfully). It was that the whole experience made me realise how limited my life is now and how vulnerable I can feel in certain situations because of my illness. For example, on the day we were travelling home, I felt so unwell that I wasn't sure I would make it through the journey and not having him there to look after me made things even worse.

I also felt very guilty that my friend couldn't do more of the things I knew she enjoyed because of my limitations (like staying out later than I could in the evenings). But I'm glad I went. We did have fun and I'm very grateful to my friend for allowing me that opportunity to test my limits. Of course, that wasn't the purpose of the trip. There was nothing intentional about it in that way. I just wanted some sun, sea and sand – as did she.

I think one thing in particular that I learned from that experience was how much my husband supports me when I don't even realise he's doing it and how safe I feel with him, to the point that I can push past boundaries I wouldn't otherwise be able to cross. He's learned about my illness alongside me and he knows what to do and how our day-to-day life needs to look. This is a good thing, because as someone who has always been big on self-reliance, it makes me feel like I'm more independent than I actually am.

For living with long-term illness – and I mean LIVING, not just existing – I think the key is finding the right balance of independence and support from others. To refuse offers of help would leave me in a very lonely and isolated place, and thankfully my pride doesn't take up so much space that I can't see past it. However, I do have to admit that being reliant on others for things I used to do without a second thought can feel demeaning, like I've taken a step back in life. But if the alternative is not going where I want to go or doing what I want to do, then the better decision is to swallow the discomfort and accept the help.

For me, a little embarrassment that I can't do certain things for myself will always come second to taking part in life. I think the reason for this is that I've experienced what it's like to be just existing (thankfully only for a short period but that was enough) and I can see exactly how my world could have closed in on me completely if I hadn't fought my way back. I don't ever want that.

Getting the balance right is tricky and it's very personal. The boundaries also constantly change for me based on how I'm feeling day to day and what part of my body is malfunctioning (and to what extent). I find that it's best to keep checking in with myself on where I'm at – can I manage myself or do I need X, Y or Z help? And I'll normally always lean towards doing something independently unless I really can't, or I know that it will set me back or put me at risk.

Food for thought...

- Where are you on the independence vs dependence scale with your illness? If you're a visual person, you could try noting it down. Draw a line on a piece of paper and put 'Fully independent' at one end and 'Fully reliant on others' at the other end, then consider where you think you sit and mark it with an 'X'

- What impact do you think your position on that scale has on your quality of life?

- Are there any small changes you could make that would allow you to feel more independent or that could help you get more out of life by accepting help?

18

Who's in the driver's seat?

Keeping a sense of control in my life

An area that I've found it helpful to put some focus on while battling long-term illness is 'control'. By this, I mean 'What do I have control over in my life?' and 'How can I feel in control?'. This subject has some overlaps with the previous chapter on independence and asking for and accepting help, but it's a topic I want to cover separately and hopefully you'll see why.

Having limited amounts of physical and mental stamina, I've found that it's more important than ever to use my energy effectively. If I were to spend most of my time getting worked up over the state of the NHS and how I'm not getting the help I need, whether I'll ever get better, why a certain friend hasn't replied to my message and how annoying it is that someone I care about won't listen to my advice, I'd be depriving myself of the opportunity to have a better quality of life.

Now, this is the moment where I need to fess up. I can get caught in unhelpful thought patterns like these, and – I'm going to sound like I'm on auto-repeat here – this is most likely to happen on a bad day with my illness. But over time I've become much better at recognising when I'm doing this and stopping myself from getting bogged down. Because it's a negative habit that can't lead to a good outcome. If I'm wasting too much mental energy on something I have no control over, it's a one-way ticket to deep frustration and feelings of injustice and powerlessness. So, my goal is to focus as much of my energy as possible on the things I can control, and by doing this, I am helping myself LIVE.

Through running training/wellbeing sessions throughout my career, I've often heard people express a sense of powerlessness in their jobs, to the point that they believe they have no control over anything. My role during these moments was to help them understand that they do – but over the smaller things, which include how they choose to react to what's going on around them. The same applies in the context of chronic illness. I absolutely understand how it feels to have the rug pulled from under you. To go from being in a relatively good place in life to feeling fit for the scrapheap. I'm saying that in a metaphorical sense, of course, and from the point of view of nothing working in my body as it should. Because no matter how awful I've felt, I know that I have something to offer the world. And while I may not be able to live my life in the way that I'd like, I do have control over many aspects of it.

Let's home in on that then – where most of my focus should be. The things that I have control over are:

- Acceptance of my illness – not taking on a victim mentality or becoming defined by it, but acknowledging that I have it, how it has changed me/my life and finding some peace with that

- Understanding who I am and what my needs are – both medical and non-medical

- My attitude towards my illness – making sure I have a positive mindset, which includes keeping my focus on what I can do, not what I can't

- My behaviours – again, trying to keep these positive and helpful

- Taking decisions about my life and my health – e.g. I decided to be a writer as that fits well within the limitations of my lifestyle, and I decided not to let my illness beat me

- Having enjoyment in my life – going for walks with my husband, doing gentle swimming (which also helps with my pain), ensuring I have some kind of social life, my writing also ticks this box

- Finding and deploying coping strategies that help me live the fullest life that I can

That's actually quite a list, which means that I do have control over many things that influence my quality of life. And in case you haven't noticed, all the above examples are covered in some shape or form within this book, whether they have a dedicated chapter of their own or they're covered within a bigger topic.

I'd say that, these days, I'm better at keeping my focus on the things I can control, but I'm not perfect – no one is. When I falter, I don't beat myself up, I show myself some of the kindness and compassion I talked about earlier in Chapter 11, *Keep your chin up*, and I work to get back on track.

Food for thought...

- Where is your focus day-to-day – is it on the things you can control or the things you can't? You might find it useful to note these down on piece of paper or in your notepad app on your phone.

- Looking at or thinking about your answers to the above question, is this way of living helping or hindering you?

- What changes could you make to shift your focus to the things you can control to improve your quality of life with your illness? Again, you can note these down so that you can come back to them later and see how you're doing.

To offer a little inspiration for the third question above, you could use strategically placed post-it notes to remind you of topics you don't want to spend too much time and energy on, or set a weekly calendar alert in your phone to remind you to look at your notes from this chapter and check in on how you're doing. Whatever works for you – the more personalised your solutions, the more likely you'll have success with them.

19

It's all about balance

Creating a more suitable and paced pattern of daily activity

Having a long-term illness that interferes with my day-to-day activities means that things I used to take for granted – like going into town – I now have to think about a bit more. It's not helpful or particularly healthy to pore over how my every move might affect me, and I certainly don't. But if I swing too far in the opposite direction, I can get caught out in ways that are unpleasant and have a negative impact (and not just in the moment). I'll share an example of this.

One day, I took a trip out for an appointment and to see to a few things in and around central Edinburgh. It required visiting three different locations that were quite far apart, so I had to think about how I would get around. Because of the distance, my first instinct was to use the bus, but I changed my mind once I was there. The weather was nice, I was enjoying myself and I like to get some physical activity each day, so I decided I would walk part of the way. I estimated that it would take me about half an hour, which on my better days is very achievable. What I didn't factor in when I made that decision was that I'd already been pottering around the shops for a while, the walk was longer than I realised (a quick check on Google Maps later told me it was actually 43 minutes) and I'd have to walk some more afterwards, even by taking the bus.

I was 15 minutes away from my destination when I ran out of energy. Now, if you suffer from fatigue, you'll know that hitting empty isn't just being a bit puffed or needing a quick sit down. It's like someone has suddenly pulled a plug, leaving you completely spent (and weak, shaky and nauseous in my case), and you don't know how you're going to make it to where you need to go. To make things worse, the route I had taken didn't allow for me to jump on a bus or hail a taxi. After resting on a bench for a while, I did eventually get there, but it was gruelling. I pushed myself way harder than I should have, and when I got home later that day, my body took revenge on me. By early evening I was experiencing a flare-up of intense pain and stiffness, and I was so fatigued that I was dragging myself around like a sack of potatoes. I had no choice but to go to bed. The next day I was the same, and it wasn't until the day after that that I began to improve. I was actually lucky that I bounced back as quickly as I did on that occasion. Sometimes it goes on for longer.

This is the part that others don't see unless they're living with someone with a condition like mine. On many occasions, I've overdone it just so I can be part of things, knowing full well the payback will come – and the people I've been out with have been none the wiser.

During the worst stages of my illness and the early stages of my (partial) recovery, I didn't know what my body was and wasn't capable of, and I've talked about how my strong achievement drive and determination tripped me up time and again. That was obviously not the way to do it. It was very much a learning curve, and I did eventually learn to pay attention and pace myself, but it took a long time to find my own personal sweet spot. These days I get caught out less frequently, and it generally happens because I'm doing better and I can forget that I need to think about these things. I consider it a good thing that my first thought isn't always, 'Can I manage that?', because it means I'm not letting my illness dictate all aspects of my life. Of course, the downside to that is finding myself in sticky situations like (or a lot more unpleasant than) the one I've described – but I'd rather that and be LIVING than lock myself away for fear of having a bad experience.

When I was rehabilitating, I had some sessions with a charity that supports people with chronic illnesses. They recognised my drive and ambitiousness (OK, my impatience too...) and the need to pace myself became a key focus in our discussions. It was one of the most the valuable moments of learning at that time, because up to that point I'd been receiving mixed messages. I mentioned earlier that some of the advice I'd had was to just push on, and there seems to be a school of thought in relation to FND that if you just ignore your symptoms and carry on as normal, you'll get better. This may work for some, but for me, as I've alluded to, it became a vicious cycle of trying to power through and being constantly knocked back.

As I learned to apply the principles of pacing, I started to make more progress. What it meant in practice was to not overdo things, particularly on a good day when my stamina is a bit better, but also not to do nothing at all on my bad days. And, believe me, it's *really* tempting to do nothing on one of those days. But as I mentioned in Chapter 10, *Why did I do that?*, I still try to do something on my worse days, and I'm often pleasantly surprised at the result.

Like so many things, it's a balancing act, and without blowing my own trumpet, I feel like I'm doing pretty well with it. There are now far more days where I get it right than where I get it wrong. So, what's my secret?

Simple rotation.

Where I am able, I rotate what I'm doing between something physical (like a household task or a walk), something cognitive (like writing or some life admin) and rest. Because – and this may be unique to my condition, so I'm not recommending it as a catch-all solution – it's quite often the case that when my mind is spent, my body is not, and vice versa. This allows me to maximise my productivity and feel like I'm achieving something. It also means I enjoy my rest time, because it feels more like a treat than a necessity.

I can also have entire days when I'm physically in bad form but my mind is clearer, or the other way around. In these situations, I'll tip the balance just a little in favour of the part of me that's doing better. But not to the point where I overdo things. Then there are days when I'm really struggling all round – physically, cognitively and with my sensory issues – and that's when I know I need to dial it back and prioritise rest.

Another important thing I've learned in relation to pacing and getting the balance right, is that I need to keep a check on how I'm doing in the moment. You might have heard the term 'listening to your body', which based on how it's worded, is suggestive of watching out for physical signs, like pain and tiredness. That's really important, and so is tuning into to my Chimp at the same time (i.e. my thoughts and feelings, as per Professor Steve Peters' model and approach). Doing this broader 'scan' allows me to pick up on additional and sometimes less obvious signs that things might not be quite right.

For example, I've already mentioned that I can get crabby and irritable when I'm running out of steam, and this happens before I'm properly aware that

I'm struggling physically or cognitively. Before I unearthed this little nugget of self-awareness, I would regularly experience what I affectionately described as 'tech-rage'. It wasn't rage – I'm not a monster. It was me getting frustrated with my poor computer for errors I was making myself, all because I had worked beyond my cognitive capacity. The mind fatigue had set in and I was trying to push through it without realising what was going on.

Identifying this 'tech-rage' issue was half the battle, and the other half was learning to sense it coming on. And I've made big strides forward. By tuning into the subtle change in my mood and cognitive decline before I get irritable, I'm generally able to prevent myself from overdoing things, or catch myself before I go over the edge.

It's not an exact science. Sometimes I'm so immersed in whatever I'm doing that I miss the signs, and sometimes I spot them and still choose not to stop because I'm enjoying what I'm doing, but I'm much more on top of this than I used to be. The same applies to physical activities. If I can tune into that subtle shift from 'hi-ho, hi-ho...' to 'this isn't quite as enjoyable or satisfying anymore', I can pare back and spare myself hours or even days of elevated fatigue, pain and other unpleasant symptoms and lost opportunities.

One final area for consideration here is work. My day job doesn't allow for me to rotate my activities in the way I've described, and I've found that to be a problem. However, I can choose which specific tasks to work on depending on how I'm feeling. For example, if I'm experiencing bad brain fog, I'll do something that takes less thinking power or that doesn't require me to read, and then I'll do the more challenging stuff when my head is clearer. My manager is also very understanding, and she's given me plenty of flexibility within the scope of what's possible. I mainly work from home, and I make sure I take a lunch break and regular screen breaks to give my eyes and brain a bit of respite. Beyond that, there's not much I can do other than keep my hours at a manageable level. Thankfully, the demands on me right now are more cognitive than physical and I'm hoping that won't change.

Food for thought...

- How well balanced is your daily activity in relation to your health needs?

- What small changes can you make to help bring better balance into your life?

20

My secret weapons

The most effective coping mechanisms in supporting my quality of life

This book is obviously jam-packed with coping mechanisms and ways in which I've navigated my illness to make sure I can have a reasonable quality of life. However, there are a few approaches I use that work so well for me, and that are so embedded in my day-to-day life, that I wanted them to feature in their own dedicated chapter. They are *distraction*, *movement and exercise* and *laughter*. I'll say a bit about each of them in turn.

Distraction

Every moment of every single day, the misfiring of signals in my body is causing all sorts of pain, discomfort, and limitation. It never goes away. It's a matter of 'volume'. Sometimes it's loud, deafening even: like my limbs are on fire, something's eating away at my bones or my chest is going to burst open. It can even be sudden shooting pains that cause me to yelp out loud. And sometimes it's more muted: just a tiresome ache or a throbbing or burning pain that nags away at me. Another of my symptoms – my nervous system being stuck in a state of 'red alert' – means that I find it difficult to relax. My brain is telling me to be 'on it' all the time, which can make me a bit hyperactive and cause me to overexert myself. That's extremely unhelpful, given that I also suffer from chronic fatigue, bouts of breathlessness, exercise intolerance and generally have very limited stamina. It really is the most paradoxical (or just plain absurd!) set of symptoms.

With all of that 'noise' going on in my body, it's hard to tune it out, and so distraction has become my number one coping mechanism. I was advised to use distraction as a specific technique to try and stop my episodes from taking over, but I've found that, as a coping mechanism, it has much broader (although sadly, not limitless) value.

Writing is a biggie in that respect. When I'm tapping away at my keyboard, creating new material or working on a heavy set of edits, I'm totally immersed in what I'm doing, and for that period I'm fully distracted from my symptoms. They haven't gone away. My focus is just elsewhere, which gives me some respite from all the unpleasantness. However, not all writing-related activities give me the same level of escape. More passive ones, such as reading back my work and lighter editing unfortunately don't give me that therapeutic benefit – in fact, they're challenging and tiring. Interestingly, this seems to correlate directly with my cognitive difficulties. The more productive/constructive (output-based) the task, the better I seem to be able to focus (unless it's a bad brain fog day and then it's 'game over'). Conversely, I really struggle with receptive (input-based) tasks like listening and reading, especially new material that I'm not already familiar with. In fact, about a year ago I made a very useful discovery linked to this issue: if I'm doing something output-based that doesn't require any active concentration, like washing dishes or cleaning the bathroom, I can listen to audio books and take in the content. That has been a joy of a discovery! I'm not a scientist, so I don't know what the explanations are for any of this, but I find it interesting all the same.

Anyway, back to distraction. Another way in which I use it as a coping mechanism – particularly when I'm out and about and I can't nip away for a rest and a lie down – is through making sure I'm in situations where my brain is engaged. What I mean by this is ensuring that I'm able to interact with others or keep myself actively occupied in some way, while avoiding passive environments where I have to listen to others for long periods without participation. Those are my kryptonite, because for some reason I can't sit quietly in a chair for any length of time without unbearable pain building up and eventually losing control of my body.

The last example I'll share on this would perhaps be 'frowned upon' by some, but I've found that watching TV is the best way of distracting my brain from my symptoms during my rest periods, especially as I struggle so much with reading and pure listening. For me, TV provides the best combination of passive and engaging to give me partial respite from the unpleasantness, while also allowing me to relax and recharge. I'm not recommending it, I'm just saying that it works for me within my own challenging health landscape. I know there are healthier ways to get physical rest, but unless you've lived in my body, please don't judge me.

Movement and exercise

Healthy habits are key to a healthy life. Of course, they are. The problem is it's hard to gain consistency with a condition that fluctuates so wildly from one day to the next, and despite my best efforts, my plans regularly come to grief or require adaption. However, even on my worst days, I still make sure that I engage in movement of some kind – even if it's just moving around my house at semi-regular intervals. Why? Because every day that I do nothing risks backwards steps.

That might sound overly dramatic, and yes, rest is important (particularly for recovery and healing), but I've found that even just a few days of almost complete inactivity can be the start of a slippery slope that's hard to climb back up. Obviously, sometimes I have no choice but to give in – especially when I catch a nasty respiratory infection – but as a rule, I won't allow myself to stop moving altogether, because I know how easy it is to lose hard won gains with stamina and therefore quality of life.

The first time I had Covid-19 it knocked me for six, but the real impact wasn't while I was testing positive for the infection itself. Surprisingly, I fared better than I expected through that part – although I was in bed for a few days, and at time, my pain became unbearable. It was post-infection where I really suffered (similar to those with Long Covid) because the infection seemed to have set me back and flared my FND symptoms in a significant way. For months afterwards, by around seven p.m. each evening, I would become very weak, nauseous and shaky and/or my body would go into meltdown with my episodes. This was extremely frustrating because I'd fought so hard to get to the point I was at before that infection, and it felt like so much of my hard work had been undone in an instant (all right, a week or two, but still…). I had no choice but to gradually work my way back again, and I did, but it took a long time, and I missed out on a lot during that period.

Of course, I had no control over that situation and it was pretty much inevitable that I would catch Covid-19 at some point, but where I do have some control, and where I know there is an element of mind over matter required, I will choose to override the messages of 'I don't feel up to this' or 'I can't face it'. I'll get my body moving, just enough to not lose what I've built up. Whether it's some household tasks such as doing the dishes, cleaning a sink or a few steps outside, making myself do something will always be better than lying around, losing stamina by the day, unless I'm struggling so badly that it'll do more harm than good. 'Use it or lose it' is the saying and I find this to be very true.

From an exercise perspective I'm lucky in that I can do a little, but there's a boundary that I can't seem to cross – and believe me, it's not from a lack of trying. Having finally managed to fine-tune my exercise routine so that I do enough but without benching myself for days, my sweet spot, it transpires, is two gentle swims of about 15 minutes twice a week (plus travel to and from the pool) and around a 30-minute walk on the other days of the week.

Full disclosure: these activities are not always easy. Walking on flat ground is generally fine and at times I can even go at a pace, but hills – even small ones – are my nemesis, and at the pool, it's often gruelling, painful and like I'm swimming through treacle. It's not a failsafe schedule either – there are days where I find these activities too challenging and have to pare back, and days where I don't manage them at all – but I do my best to stick to it. And especially because I've discovered there's a double benefit to swimming. I find the cool water to be very therapeutic for my pain (especially burning pain), so I spend some time just relaxing in it, letting it ease things for me temporarily.

At times the idea of moderate movement or exercise can seem daunting, even an impossibility, but I've heeded a key message from sessions I had with a neuro-psychotherapist back in 2015. She told me that the human body can withstand more than we think it can, so I work on the basis that I can push myself just a little bit beyond what I think I can manage, and most of the time I do OK with that. I just can't get cocky or everything quickly comes crashing down around me.

Laughter

I'm going to reference another old saying now: that laughter is the best medicine. Do I agree? Damn right, I do. But not in the sense of it making me better, because it doesn't. It's not a cure. I know this because there is *a lot* of laughter in my life. Maybe this is partly because I'm Scottish. Having a dry sense of humour is something of a feature up my way, and many of the people I spend time with have 'a bit of funny' about them.

I also have the advantage of being well-matched with my husband on the humour front. Not that many people get to see that side of him. Our lives have plenty of serious moments and moments where we have to deal with life's challenges, but aside from that, we have bucketloads of fun together. Even when I'm having a really bad day, I guarantee he'll have me snickering, chuckling or full-on belly laughing at least a handful of times. Then there's the fact that I write books with humour in them (and yes, I do laugh at my own jokes and I'm not ashamed to admit it).

Another way in which I get my daily dose of laughter is through TV. I love stand-up comedy, funny films and a good sitcom (*Friends* has been one of my staples over the years with a lot of repeat viewing). In fact, I like stand-up comedy so much that one of my books is set during the Edinburgh Fringe festival, and it's about a woman who meets a broke stand-up comedian and offers him her spare room so he can keep doing his shows.

Laughing doesn't take away the pain and discomfort of my symptoms, but it does act as a constant reminder that I am LIVING and I'm still enjoying life despite the difficulties I face each day. It also acts as an escape – however brief – from those symptoms, so perhaps it also deserves acknowledgement as an effective distraction technique.

I'm in my mid-forties now, but I truly believe that we're never too old to be playful and have fun. What is life otherwise? Hard work and endless daily responsibilities? Being serious, suave and sophisticated? Each to their own, of course, but that's not me. My body might make me feel like I'm much older than I am, but my ability to have a good time and to laugh (a lot!) really balances things out.

There's one final thing I'd like to cover as part of wrapping up this section. You may have noticed that I haven't included sleep, mindfulness or relaxation as part of my coping repertoire and there's a reason for this – one that's very personal to my situation. Like many people (and especially people who are unwell), I don't function well without enough sleep. Being sleep deprived hugely aggravates my symptoms, and while I'm almost like clockwork in getting to sleep at night (thanks to being so exhausted by the end of each day!), staying asleep is another thing altogether. I often wake up between three a.m. and five a.m., either in pain or because I'm building up to one of my episodes. I also have unrefreshing sleep, so I generally start each day feeling very drowsy, sore and like I've spent the night belting round the countryside in my very own episode of *Survivor*. On top of all that, I can't sleep during the day or on any mode of transport, and if I do try to have an afternoon nap, I just lie there feeling horrible until I give up and get up again.

I joke that the *The Princess and the Pea* is my life because of the issues my pain sensitivity causes me in bed, but laughing aside, my relationship with sleep is a difficult one. All of this unfortunately means that sleep is not a secret weapon I can deploy to help me, and along a similar vein, neither is relaxation or mindfulness. I've tried both, multiple times, but without any real benefit. Like my issue with afternoon naps, they're techniques that put additional focus on what's going wrong in my body and that's not a nice or therapeutic experience, not matter how hard I try to breathe through the pain and unpleasant sensations. I'm fully bought into the idea of their value though, and I know that they work for many others – I just wish I could benefit from them too.

Food for thought...

Coping mechanisms and how well they work will very much depend on your individual symptoms, the severity of your illness and your life circumstances. What doesn't work for one person might be another's saving grace.

- What are your main coping mechanisms and how well are they working for you?

- What other 'secret weapons' might you be able to kit yourself out with to help you live a fuller life?

<h1 style="text-align:center">21</h1>

What's the worst that could happen?

Re-building my confidence in my body

Aside from the intrusive symptoms I experience every day, one of the biggest impacts of my illness has been on my confidence – and specifically my confidence in my body. That's not to say that other aspects of my self-belief haven't been affected at all, but generally, I'm still comfortable with who I am, I still have faith in my abilities and I'm just as confident as I always was around others (both at work and in my personal life).

As we go about our lives, we tend to assume that our bodies will work as they're designed to. I took it for granted that mine would. Until it didn't. Even the health events I experienced when I was in my teens and twenties didn't rock that aspect of my confidence too much. However, since 2014 – as you'll probably have gathered by now – the functioning of my body has been completely unpredictable. Every day is different. Some days I get up and I feel not too bad, then within a couple of hours, or later that day, I can be overcome with intense pain, brain fog, crushing fatigue and/or 'wonky' senses. The opposite can also happen. I have days that start off horribly, where I'm fit for nothing, then things improve and by the evening I feel a lot better. And as I mentioned in the last chapter, when I talked about not including sleep as one of my 'secret weapons', I can have nights where I wake at 3 a.m. or 5 a.m. and lose control of my body. More often than not, these nights are followed by bad days because the lack of sleep makes my already elevated symptoms much worse. But not always.

This unpredictability hasn't just impacted my ability to live a satisfying life and get things done, it has stripped me of the faith that my body will hold up when I most need it to. I've had my episodes of uncontrollable shaking and muscle spasms in public more times than I care to think about. Thankfully I do get some warning before them – I'll start to feel weak, shaky and a bit sick. I also never know when I'm going to wake up and find myself unable to function properly (or at all). For the most part, it doesn't matter that much if I'm in bad form on a particular day. I tend to work from home, and on my bad days I can push through and still get a lot done (that's my coping technique of *distraction* in practice – I focus on my job rather than how rubbish I feel), but it does get to me when I miss the moments in life that I most want to be part of.

I love catching up with friends, but in a social context I am unreliable – through no fault of my own, I must add. I can't predict whether the date we put in the calendar will turn out to be one of my better days or a complete bust. It's like a cruel game of roulette, and quite frankly, I don't want to play anymore. The problem is, if I don't play, then I don't win on the days that do work out and I get to enjoy the company of the people I love for a few relatively carefree hours. I say, 'relatively carefree', because even if I make it along to a social catch-up or appointment – whatever it happens to be that day – I'm always battling my symptoms throughout. I might struggle to take in what someone's saying during a conversation, or I might be trying to pare myself back from talking like a runaway train because my central nervous system's 'red alert' status is at 'near critical levels'. And there will always come a point where my pain, stiffness and/or other unpleasant bodily sensations will build up and have me fighting off one of my episodes. Of course, the people I'm with will normally know nothing of this unless I have no escape route and it's game over. I generally find it best not to tell them that I'm struggling to keep the focus (and pressure) off, then as soon as I'm able, I'll make my excuses and head for home, often finding myself in difficulties on the way. But hey-ho, such is life.

It's been a learning curve, trying to re-build my faith in my body. Identifying and managing some obvious triggers that worsen my symptoms, such as avoiding caffeine and making sure I get a seat on public transport, has given me back some confidence. But some triggers I have no influence over (like infection/fever and PMS), so when they're in the mix, that little bit of confidence I've gained wavers.

As I mentioned briefly in Chapter 17, *The world is (no longer) my oyster*, I learned quickly that a total loss of confidence in my body would lead to my world closing in on me and a life of loneliness and isolation. There was no way I was giving in to that, so I've basically adopted the attitude of 'What's the worst that could happen?', and I apply this mindset to keep myself moving forward and LIVING. However, I only do so in a way that will, at its worst, lead to some discomfort and embarrassment, and not where I could be putting myself in harm's way. Because there's a difference between being brave and stretching my limits and being irresponsible and reckless. I'm aware that I'm more vulnerable than someone with no health concerns, so I won't put myself in a situation where I feel too far out of my depth.

For example, many women feel unsafe walking home alone at night/in the dark. At times, when I was younger and I went on nights out, I was one of them, and that was when I was in reasonably good health. These days, if I were to find myself in a dangerous situation in that type of environment, I wouldn't be able to run or fight back, so I don't walk down dark alleyways alone (I don't really mean dark alleyways specifically, that's very cliched, but hopefully you get my point). Plus, if I were to regularly push myself way past my limits, my poor husband would feel the brunt through constantly having to bail me out of the 'scrapes' I'd get myself in. So, when I say 'What's the worst that could happen?', what I mean is that my sweet spot for growing my confidence in my body is taking some steps out of my comfort zone so that I can do the things I want to do without getting cocky. To quote the bestselling book by the late Susan Jeffers, I 'feel the fear and do it anyway' – to a point.

Naturally, I take more 'risks' when I'm with my husband. He opens up my world that bit further so that I can see family and friends who aren't within easy reach and I can still travel (within reason). He also encourages me to keep taking part in life – not that I need much encouragement when it comes to seeing my favourite people or the temptation of sun, sea and sand. When I'm with my husband, I know that I'm in safe hands, and that allows me to have the experiences that I'd otherwise miss out on. He's been with me through every dip and sharp curve on this rollercoaster, and while he openly admits that he doesn't (and can't) properly understand how it feels to be in my body, he gets that there are invisible boundaries that I can't push beyond. When I become weak, shaky and nauseous or my body misbehaves while we're out and about or travelling (which happens regularly), he looks after me without mollycoddling me. He's practically minded, and that's exactly the kind of person I need around me during those challenging moments. When I run out of steam on holiday, he's on it straight away to find me a seat, make sure I have some water or sugar and figure out the quickest (and least demanding) way to get back to our accommodation. I feel incredibly lucky to have him in my life, and I'm more than aware of how quickly the walls would come in on me if he weren't around.

Of course, there are aspects of my life that my husband can't help with – one of which is work. Losing my confidence in my body has affected my career. I'm not a big-headed person and there are lots of things that I'm not good at, but I know I'm good at my job. However (and I cover more about this in Part Three), my relationship with my career hasn't been the same since I found my way back into the workplace. Having the skills, knowledge and experience just isn't enough if you don't have the physical or mental stamina for endless meetings and office politics. Especially when something as basic as sitting in a long meeting leaves me fighting to keep control of my body. As a result, I've finally put my corporate ambition to bed. It's a world that's incompatible with mine, so I now have to view things in a different way. I'll do the best job I can when I'm at work and that's it. I'm also proud that I'm still able to do my job given how much my illness tries to derail it.

In terms of other aspects of my confidence and self-esteem, I'm relieved that they haven't suffered too much, because I suspect that, for many people with chronic illness, that might not be the case. Perhaps it's because mine was quite strong from the outset, but I reckon that's only part of the picture. My amazing husband and family have also obviously made a difference, in that they've continually cheered me on and reminded me of how far I've come since those darker days. But I think the biggest thing has been how I've used my time and limited energy.

Where I can, I now make a point of removing myself from situations and relationships that hurt me or continually lower my mood. I'm also on the fence about social media. It has clear benefits, like connection with others; however, I think the very nature of it makes us feel bad about ourselves. By that, I mean the endless posts, reels and videos by content creators who make out they're living a better life than us (are they *really*, though?) and the ads that prey on our vulnerabilities.

And don't even get me started on the AI slop that's flooding my news feeds. The way I see it, emotional energy comes from the same tank as physical and mental energy, so it's important that I don't drain my precious resources through focusing on things that don't contribute positively to my quality of life. I'll admit though – like I have with other things – that I can still have off moments in this respect, but I experience far less FOMO these days (my age probably helps with this – I just don't care about that stuff as much anymore). Also, as I talked about in Chapter 8, *The art of self-discovery*, to feel good about ourselves we need a sense of purpose. While I've lost my way with my corporate career, I've found what I need through writing, and I believe that (aside from some moments of self-doubt due to the tough nature of the publishing industry) this has played a significant part in my continued self-belief.

Food for thought...

- What aspects of your confidence and self-belief have been impacted by your illness?

- What or who could help you re-build some of the confidence and self-belief you've lost?

On first look, the second question might seem a bit daunting, especially if you're experiencing significant levels of disability with your illness. Think about what you're good at, what you have to offer the world, what makes you feel good about yourself and what you enjoy – anything that used to be a positive in your life that you don't do much of anymore or at all. You can also consider where you might be able to push your boundaries ever so slightly to grow your confidence in your body (if that's an issue for you, like it is for me). Is there someone solid in your life who could help you with these areas you identify if you don't feel able to try them out alone? You could even ask that person for their view, as often others can see opportunities that we ourselves can't.

22

Seize the day

Having the will to keep going

Battling against long-term illness takes *a lot* of energy. Sometimes it can quite literally feel like the life is being sucked out of me, and I've voiced at times that I feel decades older than I am. Thankfully, my motivation to keep fighting to maintain the quality of life I've reclaimed is strong, and I have the determination to get up and do something productive each day – even on the bad ones. However, there *are* moments where I feel overwhelmed and like I can't continue this way indefinitely. I find it hard to believe that there's anyone with a debilitating chronic condition who doesn't feel like this occasionally.

When I have better days, I make sure I acknowledge them to keep myself moving forward in a positive frame of mind – and I've found that music is a helpful tool for doing this. In the early days of my rehabilitation, when I was battling to get some semblance of my previous life back, it was all about small steps and staying focused on my recovery. I experienced so many health-related setbacks at that time (and still do, but thankfully to a lesser extent), so when I felt like I was making good progress, I'd stick my earphones in and listen to *Proud* by Heather Small while doing a bit of cleaning or taking a short walk. It's such a powerful and emotive track and it would act as a clear reminder of the progress I'd made while motivating me to keep going.

Having something to feel proud of or good about, no matter how small and trivial, gives me reason to look forward to tomorrow. Moments of pride don't need to be big and PR-worthy. They can come from managing to cope physically with something I didn't expect to. They can be about reflecting on a time when things were worse and how – through my own perseverance – I've improved. Or they can stem from achieving more than I thought I would on any given day (without pushing myself too hard and overdoing things). With a significant health challenge, I think it's important to acknowledge how big an achievement the tiniest of steps forward can be and I talk about this more in the next chapter.

From a motivational perspective, we're all different. We can find our get-up-and-go through things that make us feel good or proud, such as learning something new, having an enjoyable experience or helping another person. Or we might need to promise ourselves a reward of some sort to help us find our mojo. It's about knowing what works for you. In addition to music, I get energised by spending time outdoors (even just sitting quietly on a bench for a few minutes), doing something creative that gives me a feeling of achievement (my writing) or having something to look forward to (a family get-together, a holiday or something fun I have planned with my husband). And if I'm seeking the motivation to do something necessary but unappealing, especially on one of my worse days, I do dangle a carrot to get myself going. This is normally the promise of a (small) tasty treat – especially if the thing I need to do is physically demanding – or the next episode of a favourite series. Knowing what energises me and what will kickstart me when I'm on a low ebb means that I can deploy these tactics to make sure I'm LIVING and not allowing the emotional part of my brain to rule me and steal away my opportunities (remember Professor Steve Peters' Chimp?). And if that doesn't work or it's a *really* bad day, then perhaps it's time to just bunker down with a good box set and be kind to myself.

Food for thought...

- What gets you out of bed each day and keeps you motivated?

- What moments of pride have you experienced with your illness? If you can't think of any, could it help to start looking out for these opportunities to keep you moving forward?

- What could help you feel more motivated to make the most of each day? *

Acknowledging that we'll all have days where we're just too unwell or don't feel able to keep going.

23

Move those goal posts

Redefining ambition and success

'Success' and 'failure' are probably two of the most politically charged words in society. Every day, the media reports on what feels like endless failures in all corners of life. There are fewer reports of successes, but when they come, they come with lots of fanfare and positive accolades. On the face of it the definitions of these words seem objective. Success means something has gone well. Failure means something has not gone well or gone badly. But is that the only way to look at it? It turns out not.

One of my biggest moments of personal growth came nearly twenty years ago when I was hungry for career development and a more experienced colleague kindly offered me the opportunity to go through my first emotional intelligence self-assessment. I jumped at this. After I'd completed it, I had a feedback session with this colleague, the purpose of which was to take me through my results to help me digest them and identify some related development goals.

During my feedback session, I talked a lot about how I wanted to be successful. Back then I was still a bit green behind the ears, and I was keen as mustard to make my mark on the world (anyone thinking of Cluedo right now? Because I am). Anyway, this colleague picked up on my drive to be successful and she asked me, 'What does success mean to you?'. Well, I was thrown. I thought it was obvious. I wanted to do well in my career, work my way up the ladder, earn a big salary – surely that was how I would be able to consider myself a success? She then asked me why I saw that as the definition of success. Was that what I really wanted or had I learned that from elsewhere? Now, my memory of our exact conversation is a bit woolly, but what I do remember is this: it turned out that my definition of success was based on the societal influences in my life. To be successful I had to have a good job, lots of money, a house with a white picket fence (I'm kidding, I know that's the American dream but are we all that different here in the UK?).

This colleague had given me something to think about, and essentially, where I eventually landed with it was that success has to *mean something to me*. It has to be mine, I have to view it as important (like properly – not because I think I should see it that way) and it has to be something that I can feel genuinely good about.

Looking at that life lesson through different eyes – the eyes of someone with chronic illness – it has been an important question for me to revisit in recent years. I can't do many of the things I might have done if I'd stuck with that generic definition of success. If I hadn't moved the goalposts to an entirely different playing field, I might have been sitting here feeling like a failure right now, and I probably wouldn't have written this book, or any books at all.

OK, so I don't have a high-flying career and I don't bathe in the oodles of money I've not made, but figuring out my own definition of success has resulted in me achieving things that that I might never have expected to. Things that make me feel good – even if others don't value them. I learned that having status, a fancy job title and money aren't my main drivers in life, and thank goodness for that, because it would have been one hell of a clash with my current health predicament.

So, what about failure? Isn't failure always something that's gone badly or hasn't worked out? Something to feel ashamed of? I suppose it is if you want to see it that way. But I like the attitude that we can never fail as long as we've tried. Every 'failure' is a learning opportunity, and if we can take something from it, how can it be an entirely negative thing? I've worked on various personal projects over the last ten or so years. Have they all led to great success using the societal definition of the word? No, they haven't. So, are they failures? I don't think so. Because I've enjoyed working on them and I've learned new skills and things about myself along the way, and they've helped shape who I am today.

Success with a long-term illness looks and feels quite different to success without one. Something I've had to keep reminding myself of is that I can't keep up with others who are in sparkling (or at least decent) health and I shouldn't even be trying to. That's unfortunately one of the many downsides of having a (mainly) non-visible illness. Most of the time I don't look unwell, which means that people forget that I can't keep up. They might even question if my illness is real, because there are some things I can do and some I can't – and some of it doesn't even make sense to me, so what chance do others have of figuring it out?

I don't want to be treated differently, but at the same time I need to be treated differently. If the set-up of my day job was the same as it is for others without a disability, I'd soon find myself in difficulties and sinking fast. The same principle applies to my own personal goals and measures of success. I can't run a marathon (or even a few hundred yards for that matter), I'm not going to be a big gun in the corporate world and I'm probably never going to be able to tour the world. The big shiny goals that require a fully functioning body aren't even worth thinking about. But big goals aren't off the table altogether, as I've discovered, having now published several women's fiction/romcom novels and this book. They just have to align with the capabilities I do have and be something I can chip away at gradually, in my own time. And I have to really want to achieve them.

Probably unsurprisingly, I find that setting big goals while living with a debilitating illness piles on a layer of pressure that just isn't helpful. When I start a new book, the idea of writing eighty to ninety thousand words is daunting, and that's after having written quite a few. I may know that I can do it, but when I'm in pain and struggling to think or read back my work through terrible brain fog, it feels like an impossible task. What I do to overcome that is bargain with myself. 'Sit down and try to write two-hundred words, and if you're not feeling well enough, then at least you tried.' That's what I tell myself (it's another of Professor Peters' Chimp management tactics), and most of the time I write way more than those two hundred words. In fact, I get so into the flow of writing that I forget I even made that deal with myself in the first place.

For me, the goals need to be bite-sized (though they can absolutely add up to something bigger) and success needs to be celebrated along the way, not just at the finishing line. Not because I'm ego driven or anything, but because it's a way of building confidence in my physical and mental ability to do the things I aspire to and of feeling like I'm achieving something. For this very book, I set up a progress tracker with all the different chapter headings and ticked each one off as I completed it. It made the process of writing it a lot less intimidating, and every time I checked something off it was a mini success. And this approach doesn't just apply to my writing. Small successes in a different context might be managing a longer walk without my body biting back hard, travelling one leg of a trip abroad without coming to grief, or getting through a month without a really bad day (oh, I wish! Let's say a fortnight).

Re-setting and continually reviewing my criteria for a successful life (in my eyes, not anyone else's) and celebrating smaller achievements has become a core part of my lifestyle that has been key to feeling like I can keep fighting on. Because if I know that I'm on the right track (for me) and I'm winning, even in the smallest way, then I'm giving myself more opportunity for a better quality of life.

Food for thought...

- What goals do you set yourself and how achievable are they?

- What does success mean to you and could you benefit from thinking about it differently? Remember what I said about having a definition of success that means something to you, not what others or society might expect of you.

- How do you look at failure? Could you reframe this?

- What were your last three successes? Ask yourself this question regularly if you want to get in the habit of being your own biggest supporter.

24

Follow the trail of breadcrumbs

Keeping myself on track

There's one final quick area I'd like to cover before moving onto Part Three. This section of the book (Part Two) has been about the benefits I've gained through looking inwards – getting to know myself, helping myself and becoming my own biggest supporter.

It's too easy to feel a sense of hopelessness – even pointlessness – when struggling against an unrelenting illness, and sometimes I feel like I'm in a losing battle. But the best question I can ask myself at those rare points when I feel it's all too much is: 'What's the alternative?'. While I'm still fighting on, I'm offering myself a chance at the best quality of life I can have. No one else is going to do that for me, and if I give up, I know the only way I'm headed is downhill – and probably quite fast.

I don't want to lose all the gains I've made. And I certainly don't ever want to experience the events of 2014 again (if I can avoid that) so my mission is simple: I need to keep my head up and keep working on me. It's a task without an ending – like a video game with infinite levels – so I have to view it a bit like housework. It can be a pain, but it's necessary, and I'll feel better for it.

Each positive change I make and each unpleasant experience I have provides me with feedback. It tells me something about how I'm doing: whether I'm keeping on track or losing my way. Like following a trail of breadcrumbs, I use those clues to identify what I need to look at and address next.

Food for thought...

- What experiences have you had recently that give you 'intel' on how you're doing?

- How can you use that information to help you keep moving forward?

Part Three
Dealing with the outside world

25

Scanning the horizon

A perspective for dealing with the outside world

In Part Two, the focus was on how I look inwards at myself – how I hold up the mirror, so to speak, and work hard to gain the best quality of life I can through self-reflection and small changes to how I live. In this next section (Part Three), I'm shifting the focus to looking outwards at others and the outside world, including the social side of things and the workplace. However, looking outwards *doesn't* mean that I stop self-reflecting. If you remember from Chapter 18, *Who's in the driver's seat?*, we can't control others or the environments we find ourselves in, but we can control how we respond to and interact with people, as well as how we navigate our way through life's challenges. If this isn't fresh in your mind, I'd suggest going back and re-reading that chapter before diving into this section.

We all hope for fair treatment and respect, but the reality of chronic illness is that, at some point, you're likely to experience ignorance, prejudice and the unpleasant impacts of stigma (whether intentional or not) – and if you don't, I expect that you're in the lucky minority. I have no solid evidence on which to base that assumption, but because of my openness about my illness, people often share their own bad experiences and/or those of their loved ones with me. This includes the comments that too easily slip out of other people's mouths and that anecdotal feedback is hard hitting.

Sadly, it seems like prejudice (whether intended or not) is par for the course, and I believe that it's better to be ready for it than to expect fair treatment wherever you go and feel let down. To be clear, I'm not excusing ignorance and bad behaviour, and I do call it out where I see it (at times). But as well as being 'a big supporter of the cause', I live my life with a sizeable dollop of realism. Being prepared for bias, prejudice and stinging remarks is a way of 'building my coat of armour' – the idea of which I introduced in Chapter 14, *When the going gets tough*, in Part Two. It means that when I experience them, they don't hurt me in the way that they might if they were to come as a shock. Especially as they can just as easily come from the people I love as medical professionals, people I don't know and those I'm only acquainted with through work or other aspects of my wider life. That's not to say that the people I love would intentionally hurt me. I know they wouldn't. They're always well-meaning, but their words and actions may not always be well-chosen, well-informed and/or land how they intend them to. When that happens, I might to educate them 'with love'. Or if I don't want to get into it, I'll just let it wash over me. It's very tiring trying to be an 'activist' and often I just don't have the energy for it.

How we view the outside world and how we choose to engage with it and those around us is just as important as looking inwards at ourselves. As with Part Two, in this section I've shared my experiences under different topics, and you'll find the same *Food for thought* questions at the end of each chapter (apart from one – the next one – all will become clear). The aim of these is to help you think about how you can get into that driver's seat and aim for positive experiences, all while protecting yourself.

26

From hero to zero

Losing my sense of worth in the eyes of others

OK, I'll admit the title of this chapter is a little misleading in the sense that I was never anyone's hero (not that I know of anyway) but bear with me and all should become clear.

From a work perspective, prior to my FND derailing my life, I was an employee who was considered a solid (or even high) performer. I was ambitious, I was focused and driven, and I'd delivered a number of challenging projects successfully. Things were looking bright in terms of my future career.

As I touched on in my story in Part One, after Christmas 2013, when it became clear that whatever was going on with my health during that period hadn't passed, I did what I expect most people who haven't received any answers would do. I tried my best to ignore the strange symptoms I was experiencing and just pushed on. This worked as a general coping strategy when my health issues were simmering at a low level, but as time progressed it felt like my body was acting out a physical interpretation of Dr Jekyll and Mr Hyde. I had days when I felt good, energised and motivated. On those days, I enjoyed by my job, I was ambitious and I wanted to keep building my career. However, that feeling never lasted, because there were too many days in between where I'd wake up feeling fatigued and foggy headed, and I'd have the same tremulous feeling in my core that I experienced during Christmas 2013. On those days my confidence (in my body, not my professional abilities) would dip, and I couldn't imagine being able to sustain long-term in the role I already had, never mind make any sort of upward move in the company. This left me playing an endless game of ping-pong in my mind in relation to my career aspirations, which was both confusing and frustrating.

At that time my department was in the early stages of a restructure, which included the opportunity to apply for voluntary redundancy. While I did want a challenging role in the new set-up, and my performance was thankfully as solid as it had always been, there was a part of me that was wondering if I should jump ship while I had the chance. I was becoming increasingly concerned that I needed to seek proper medical help, and a financial package and some time out/a slower pace of life would allow me the space to do that. I felt deeply conflicted and there was no easy answer – both options had big pros and cons. In the end, the part of me that was hanging onto my career aspirations won, and I decided not to put my hand up for voluntary redundancy.

It wasn't long after that when I experienced the violent episode at work and had no choice but to take time off. At that point, in a moment of desperation and concerned that I was about to end up off sick long-term, I asked one of my managers if they would allow me to submit a late application to leave the company on voluntary redundancy. This request was denied.

It was a strange time, and of course there were other dynamics at play in my workplace – it wasn't an entirely one-dimensional scenario – but I won't go into these, because they're not relevant to the key focus of this chapter. What is relevant is that I was experiencing what, looking back, felt like a painfully elongated fall from 'dizzy heights' (not that I was particularly senior, but hopefully you get what I mean). It was kind of like the world's longest and slowest sky dive – and I didn't know if my parachute was going to open. I had been trying my best to keep going, but deep down I knew something was very wrong and eventually I hit the ground with a thud (quite literally, actually, many times).

As I also mentioned in my story in Part One, I hoped that a couple of weeks off work might help and allow me to get back to being the able professional that I knew I was. The conversations with my manager at that point were focused on them wanting to support me and hoping to see a swift return. I still felt like a valued member of the team. But as it became clear that this was not something that was going to pass quickly, and I was signed off work for a longer period, the tone towards me soon changed.

I observed this shift with dismay as, in the eyes of my employer, I evolved from being a desirable employee to a problem absence case. That hurt like hell and it most certainly didn't help my recovery. Unfortunately, unless a person has experienced a life-changing illness themselves (or watched it happen to someone they care about), they have limited capacity to understand how awful it is to be so unwell, and on top of that, to be treated like you're no longer of use. I didn't blame my manager – they were just doing what they were told to do to comply with what was company policy at that time, but the impact was significant.

Hopefully, the title of this chapter now makes more sense. Essentially, I felt like I'd gone from being a career woman with real potential to being chucked on the corporate rubbish heap. I was no longer an effective resource in their eyes, and they were more than ready to cross me off their payroll. I even remember at one point having a very uncomfortable conversation with my manager, who was not-so-subtly hinting that perhaps I could just resign instead of being dragged through a humiliating formal absence (capability) process. They weren't a bad person, so I like to think that they did this because they felt for me and were trying to spare me the pain. I told them in no uncertain terms that I couldn't afford to resign, and that I intended to return to work when I was able, so the formal absence meeting was put in the calendar – and it was every bit as humiliating and demeaning as I expected it to be.

I'm not unrealistic. I don't expect that an employer should support someone who is off sick indefinitely, but what I do strongly believe is that, if that person has given loyal service and they're making positive progress, they should be given a fair chance to recover without additional unnecessary stress being piled upon them. This being partly out of respect and a sense of humanity, but mainly to avoid destroying their confidence and self-esteem and sending them hurtling backwards in their recovery in the process. Thankfully, my confidence and self-esteem were able to take it in the long run, but my recovery was set back, and I can imagine many others have suffered greatly in similar circumstances.

Unsurprisingly, it took me a while to get over that experience, and equally unsurprisingly, after that first formal absence meeting, all I wanted was to get out of that place so that I could focus on what I really needed to: getting better. It was an experience that led to me reviewing my priorities and my loyalties in life.

I've talked already about how we all need a sense of purpose. We also want to feel like we belong (more on this later). Work wasn't my life, but it was a big part of it, like it is for most people – whether they're career minded or just need to pay the bills. It provided me with that sense of purpose and belonging. Until the point that my health was going downhill and I wobbled, I had shown real loyalty and gone above and beyond to deliver more than what was asked of me – and what had I been rewarded with? The painful reality that I was nothing more than a number and it felt like that number was a big fat zero. I didn't belong there anymore – that had been made clear – so it was time to look elsewhere.

Food for thought...

This chapter is less of a 'teachable moment' and more a depiction and acknowledgement of the lowest moments that can manifest when dealing with the outside world during a challenging illness. The career angle is almost irrelevant, as being made to feel like a 'zero' can happen in any area of our lives – at home, with extended family, in our friendship groups, in a learning or community setting or at work. No matter where it happens, it hurts.

This part of my story simply illustrates how a point in time can be so awful that it can feel like there's no coming back from it. But I did come back from mine, and so do others. If you've experienced something like this, I feel your pain. Just know that you're not alone and that in time you will move on from it. And it's OK to feel hurt.

27

Shame on you

Living in the shadow of a stigmatised illness

One thing that I find utterly confounding in life is the contradictions around what's accepted to be real and what's not. Too often it feels like people (and by 'people' I mean *some* people) will only accept what is convenient for them to believe in. The impact of this on someone with a long-term illness is, of course, obvious – and especially when it comes to non-visible illness.

Firstly, there's the false belief that certain illnesses aren't real or they're being made up, purely because the person doesn't look unwell and nothing shows up in the wide, but still somewhat limited, battery of medical tests that are available. Sure, it's great if they can just prick you with a needle or shove you in a machine to get the answers, but there are a lot of circumstances where it's not as straight-forward as that.

What has become clearer and clearer to me through my own experiences and hearing the accounts of others, is that medical experts can't always give an answer (and as an aside: in my opinion, it's better for them be to up front about that than to go to the 'easy answer' of anxiety or something equally unhelpful). As I touched on earlier when I was talking about FND, neuroscientists also acknowledge that there's still a lot they don't yet understand about how the brain works, which must surely mean there's more for us human beings to learn about ways in which our bodies malfunction. Unfortunately, despite this, and despite the whopping amount of evidence proving that non-visible illnesses like FND, CFS/ME, Fi-bromyalgia and Long Covid are real, the naysayers of this world (both medical and non-medical) continue to believe that if it can't be proven with tests then there's nothing wrong – you're malingering or it's all in your head.

Add to that the inability of most people who haven't lived with symptoms such as chronic fatigue and pain, brain fog, loss of co-ordination, etc, to even imagine what they feel like and how crippling they can be. It doesn't take a rocket scientist to understand why people with stigmatised illnesses have the negative experiences that they do. I can't count how many times, when people have asked me how I'm doing and I tell them that I'm experiencing quite a lot of fatigue, they reply with 'Oh, I'm tired today too' – as if what I'm describing is perfectly normal. While there is nothing intentional in a statement like this and the person doesn't mean any harm, it's still a problem, because by not even *trying* to understand the difference, the stigma associated with these illnesses perpetuates.

I've never lost a limb, but I'm capable of understanding that there would be many challenges that come with that. These would likely include significant physical and psychological impacts, some of which I could guess and others that I could not. So, if I were ever to meet someone who had experienced such a trauma and they were open about it, I would listen, try my best to understand,

show compassion and learn from them. And not because their disability might be visible to me, but because they're a person dealing with something that's real and they deserve my support and respect.

The illness that I have (FND, as a reminder) is unfortunately highly stigmatised and sadly that stigma comes from the way it's been viewed historically. It has had a series of unfortunate names such as 'hysteria', 'psychogenic illness' and 'conversion disorder'. With the latter, the suggestion is that the patient is converting psychological distress/trauma into physical symptoms. While it has now been widely accepted that this is not what's going on for a lot of people with FND (and that a person doesn't have to have depression or anxiety or be stressed to develop it either), the problem is that 'mud sticks'. That's not to trivialise or take away from the very real role that psychological trauma can play in the onset of FND for some patients or the harmful effects of psychological trauma more generally. They can, of course, be life shattering. But it's extremely unhelpful for those (like me) for whom the 'conversion disorder' interpretation isn't relevant and for whom depression, anxiety and stress haven't played a role either. It's already challenging enough having FND without these red herrings being hurled into the mix. I've experienced this issue first-hand and it's basically just another unnecessary battle that I've had to fight when I'm already wading through enough crap.

Of course, it's not just patients with FND who endure the negative effects of stigma – and if you have a long-term illness, you'll likely know this yourself. I regularly see posts and comments on posts on social media by people with various chronic illnesses who describe being treated appallingly by medical professionals who don't believe that what they're experiencing is real or that they could possibly be suffering or struggling as much as they are. They describe being accused of making it up, attention seeking, exaggerating, being neurotic... it's a long list.

I remember once having one of my episodes while at the hospital and a nurse aggressively shouting at me to 'Stop it!' and 'Calm down!'. Like, how helpful is that when my body is in meltdown? I found myself having to justify my 'behaviour' when I had no control over what was happening to me. If only I'd been able to do that without stuttering and stammering so I could have made my point more assertively. But, you know, I was kind of going through a hellish experience, and the last thing I would have expected in a situation like that was a stand-off with someone who was supposed to be offering me care.

Having a stigmatised condition (visible or non-visible) is not fun. It's the opposite of fun. Because it's hard enough just being unwell without adding in a layer of shame. A diagnosis can be a relief, but not when it means that you'll be watched by sceptical eyes or regarded as a hypochondriac. I've felt ashamed. I already admitted that when I mentioned complaining to my neurologist about having such a 'ridiculous' thing wrong with me. It's not ridiculous though. That would imply that my situation is deserving of mockery or that it's funny or entertaining in some way. And while I do have moments when I laugh about my body malfunctioning in the strangest ways, the truth is having a stigmatised illness is no laughing matter.

My visible symptoms are embarrassing. There's no getting away from it. I'm used to being stared at, but it will never feel comfortable, even if people are only looking at me with faces of concern. I don't want to be the performing monkey on whatever day things go south for me. When I'm out and about, all I want is to blend in with everyone else, but unfortunately when my FND decides it's going to be visible, it's VISIBLE. Why would *anyone* want to fake that? Writhing around on the floor like a seal on amphetamines or sitting on a bench looking and sounding like I'm being strangled by the Invisible Man. All I can do during those moments is acknowledge the embarrassment, remind myself that I have nothing to be ashamed of and push on. I know that my illness is real, and while it's embarrassing, it's a big part of my life and I can't change that. So, I just get on with things. Oh, and I thank my lucky stars that this isn't the seventeenth century, because by now I may well have been burned at the stake for being a witch.

Food for thought...

- Do you have a stigmatised condition or feelings of shame associated with your illness, and if so, how does that feel?

- What could help you push back any unpleasant feelings so you can focus on looking after you?

28

Where do I fit in?

Finding a new sense of belonging

Prior to 2014, I wasn't a party animal, but I did have an active lifestyle and a full life. I worked full-time in HR, and outside of work I would enjoy spending time with my partner, my family and friends. I'd exercise, I'd socialise a couple of times a week and I'd still have proper nights out. I was busy 'doing life', and while my somewhat unpredictable health was an obstacle at times, I'd always get back on track reasonably quickly. It was a life that I loved, and best of all, I knew exactly where I fitted in.

That sense of belonging is something that I never put enough value on, I now realise. I always knew of its importance, but it was only during the fallout from my body's spectacular meltdown and the loss of my full and active lifestyle that I realised what I'd lost. Because when I attempted to resurrect my previous life a bit at a time, I realised that the jigsaw pieces no longer fit together in the way that they did before.

I couldn't simply slot back into my job or reactivate my social life as a carbon copy of what it was. And while my partner and my family adjusted so that I could still be a central part of their lives, I couldn't expect the same of my friends and colleagues. Now, this might be the point where you're thinking that good friends and colleagues would do that for you. Yes, they would, but only to a point, and that's all I can reasonably expect from them. Relationships are two-sided and both parties need to gain from them, so if that balance is thrown too far off, they're no longer viable. I've had enough life experience to understand that, but it still doesn't feel good.

Also, as I mentioned briefly in Chapter 9, *Who am I now?* in Part Two, with all this happening in my early(ish) thirties, there were two main social angles at play: the 'new or new(ish) parents', many of whom tend to socialise only with each other where their hectic and largely sleepless lives allow, and the 'we'll party 'til someone or something stops us' crowd who were still making the most of their freedoms. I didn't fit in with either. I wasn't a parent, so I had less in common with people in that group and their limited socialising capabilities didn't match well with mine, and nights out (even just parties, wedding receptions or late dinner catch ups) had become a near impossibility for me. On the rare occasion that I've pushed myself to be part of the latter, I've either ended up having one of my episodes (in far too public a way for my liking) and had to leave early, or I've suffered the gruelling effects for days after. I'll admit that I shed some tears over that realisation of not knowing where I belonged and the feeling of isolation that came with it, but I didn't allow it to take over me. Instead, I put my limited energy into figuring out my new world.

So where did and do I fit in? Well, I've found my way back to the workplace (more on this later). I've also carved out a small but significant place for myself (at least, to me) in the world of writing and publishing. When it comes to social groups and socialising, I'm over a decade older now, so that isn't quite as important as it was, but it still holds some importance to me. So, I've created my own patchwork quilt of a social life that has restored a bit of that aspect of belonging for me.

I spend most of my spare time with my husband or resting on my own (often with Netflix or the like for company), and as someone with both introvert and extrovert tendencies, I'm fine with that. Plus, my husband is my favourite person in the world, so hanging out with him is the best fun I can have. I have a great family and a small, close-knit group of author friends who I'm in constant (virtual) contact with, and I love the feeling of belonging those friendships have re-invigorated for me. I'm also still in touch with many of my good friends who were in my life before 2014, but unfortunately most of them live at a distance I can't easily travel (and certainly not alone). I don't see much of them, but when I do it's amazing and it gives me a nostalgic glimpse into my former life. Post-my return to work, I've also made a few friends out of supportive colleagues and I really value those relationships. They haven't known me without my illness and that makes things a bit easier for me in terms of 'justifying' my needs. I know I should never feel like I have to justify anything, but it kind of comes with the territory, especially when my FND is, for the most part, non-visible.

I definitely took my old life and the sense of belonging that came with it for granted. I never expected it to be upended in the way that it was, and if I'd know what I would face, maybe I would have valued it more. But that's what we do – we just assume that we'll be able to keep slotting in where we always have – and in a way, why not? There isn't much to be gained from worrying that your place in the world might be whipped away from you at any moment. Life is for living, as the old saying goes.

Food for thought...

- How has your lifestyle changed since becoming unwell and what has that meant for your sense of belonging?

- How do you feel about the aspects that you've lost?

- If you're struggling to work out where you fit in now, what or who might help you do that? Some options might be a support group, an interests' group (a hobby of some sort) or getting involved with a charity or your community in some way (online or even in-person, if that's something you can manage). Asking someone you trust to help you dip your toe in the water might also be a way of making it feel less daunting.

29

Friends for life?

Reshaping my relationships

I covered a bit about relationships and friendships in the last chapter, but it's an important area. It can also be a tricky and sensitive one, so it deserves a chapter of its own.

There were some relationships that I lost or that evolved for me (and not in a positive way) on the back of my illness taking over in 2014. Not because those people abandoned me, but because the circumstances that linked us had changed (i.e. I was no longer working and I couldn't socialise). I won't lie, it really stung. Because I knew life was carrying on without me and that I was missing out.

However, looking back with the benefit of hindsight and wisdom, I can now see things more rationally. I felt some of those losses more deeply than I should have, and it's quite obvious and understandable why I did. I felt very isolated. But here's the thing: friendships are often a valuable (and enjoyable) by-product of a shared stage in life, such as working or studying together, sharing a hobby, maybe parenting at the same time, even meeting new people on holiday, but unless the bond runs deep these relationships will probably come to a natural end sooner or later. I have had plenty of friendships that have run their course over the years. I think what was different about that period in my life was that the friendships I lost or that changed significantly for me happened collectively and more abruptly than I might have otherwise experienced. That was always going to hurt. But at least I know now that, in the main, those losses were just premature – they were relationships that would likely have ended or changed anyway – as opposed to being 'priceless jewels' cruelly stolen away by my illness.

Someone wise once said to me that having a small number of close lifelong friends I can depend on is better than having lots of people in my life who won't be there when it counts. And they were right – quality really does trump quantity. It's perhaps in part down to my personality type (being a halfway house between introvert and extrovert), but I'd much rather sit in a café or restaurant and have meaningful conversations and great banter with a couple of good friends than hang out with a boisterous group of people whom I only ever engage with at surface level. That won't be everyone's preference but it's mine. I want the precious little time I can invest in my friendships to count.

With such limited ability to maintain my relationships, catching up with friends is not necessarily the pleasant experience that it should be. When it comes to making arrangements (especially with more than one person at a time), I feel like a pain in the backside because I can't be as flexible as other people. It's embarrassing to have to say, 'I can meet up, but only if X, Y and Z conditions are met'. I also hate asking people to come to me because it feels like I'm inconveniencing them, and when people invite me to visit them, that also comes with challenges that they simply don't understand. Then, once I've made an arrangement with someone or a small group of friends, it's down to the luck of the draw whether I'll be well enough to follow through on the day. And I *hate* letting people down. These issues can even hold me back from making plans in the first place or cause me to remove myself from a situation altogether to avoid making things difficult.

All of the above can make trying to have a social life unpleasant and feel like a chore. Especially because, once I've managed to work my way through seeing everyone I want to see, it's been so long since I saw the person I first caught up with that I have to start from the beginning again. I don't even see as much of my immediate family as I'd like to.

Sometimes I've wondered how my friends feel about my limitations and unreliability, but my hope (and expectation) is that their lives are busy enough that they don't give it much thought. What has also crossed my mind is whether the people in my life get sick of hearing about my health. Do I sound like a stuck record to them? Perhaps. My illness is a huge (and hugely restricting) part of my life in same way as their kids, jobs, etc are a significant part of theirs, so it's going to come up – a lot. I think what it ultimately comes down to is that true friends – the ones that I should focus my time and energy on – are those who will offer me unconditional support, kindness and compassion without judgement. And I'm lucky enough to have a good few of those.

I've already mentioned that I'm on the fence about social media. I also prefer to catch up with people face-to-face, however, with this having become more difficult, I've had to rely more on the likes of WhatsApp and Messenger for keeping in contact with friends and family. And thank goodness for those tech solutions, otherwise I'd probably have lost a fair few more friends by now, purely through lack of contact. Thankfully though the opposite is true, and over recent years I've found new (and important) relationships through social media – in particular, my friendship group with three other authors. We can't meet up in person, because we live in different countries and even on different continents (I really wish we could) but the virtual nature of our friendship has its benefits. No matter how rubbish I feel, I can always take part in our catch ups, and as we live in different time zones I almost always have someone to chat to – whether that be during the day or when I'm awake and struggling with my symptoms in the middle of the night.

With long-term illness, it's natural to want others to show empathy. However, something important I've learned about relationships/friendships and interacting with others generally is this: no matter how good someone's intentions are towards me, they can't fully empathise or understand my situation, and I shouldn't expect them to be able to. It would be great if people who have no significant health issues could understand (like, *really* understand) how hard it is, but that's unrealistic. It's very difficult for people to do that unless they've lived through similarly challenging circumstances themselves or they are close to someone who has.

What I do think is reasonable is to hope that those who genuinely care about me would at least try to understand and imagine how they would feel in my situation. It goes two ways, though, so I also try to put myself in the shoes of others. I do this by accepting that they can't always understand and get it right and, for example, by not expecting my friends to change their lives for me just because I can only socialise in a restricted way. Some of my friends simply can't line up with the way I have to live my life, because of family commitments or whatever, or perhaps they simply don't want to – and that's fine. I'm lucky enough to have friends who can and who choose to do so, and I really treasure those moments we get to spend together.

Empathy and consideration that goes both ways is an essential foundation for successful and meaningful relationships, as is respect, loyalty, trust and ensuring that both people in the relationship are getting something out of it. For me, this is the winning formula, and something I won't compromise on. I'm too old and lacking in energy these days to put up with anything less.

Food for thought...

- What friendships and relationships do you have in your life and are you putting your (possibly limited) energy into the ones that matter most? You could keep in mind my 'winning formula' above when thinking about this, only if you find it helpful.

- How much time and energy do you spend on friendships/relationships that are of little value to you and/or the other person?

- If you're putting too much into friendships that aren't beneficial to you and not enough into those that could be, how can you change this?

- How empathetic are you towards the people in your life who are trying, but who struggle to understand your situation and needs?

30

Family fortunes

Depending on those I could trust most

Family is an area where I've been really fortunate. Sometimes I've even joked that maybe I became unwell because I wasn't allowed to have it good all round. Obviously, that's not true, and my family isn't perfect (no one's is), but I really do feel like I lucked out in this aspect of life. When I talk about family, I mean my husband, my parents, my brothers and sisters-in-law and their kids. Their support over the last decade and a bit has been unwavering, and I really couldn't ask for more.

My husband is a man of integrity, who always thinks of others before himself. So much so that I often have to prod him to consider himself and what he needs. He's also bags of fun (I think I've already mentioned this) and our personalities line up well, despite us being quite different people. If I were to be corny, I'd say he's my partner in crime, the yin to my yang, the pepper to my salt... OK, enough of that. I'm almost reaching for the sick bowl myself. And if you're a pessimist, or even a realist, I get that this sounds too good to be true, so I'll temper things by confirming that you're right. Like other couples, we bicker, argue and get on each other's nerves at times, but when it comes to the important stuff we're very well aligned.

The reason I'm so appreciative of and thankful for the husband I have is because my situation could very well have been different. You've seen *Sliding Doors*, right? (If not, it's a great movie to snuggle under the duvet in front of.) Our paths crossed during an (online) moment in time and if anything had played out that little bit differently, I might have ended up in a much worse situation than I'm in now. And I'm not just saying that because of a blockbuster movie and chance and all. I'm saying it because I've had other relationships in my adult life where I was not a good match with the person I was with at the time, and I know that if I'd become this unwell, our partnership would have been strained to breaking point. That's not to say that they were bad men – they absolutely weren't. It's just that my husband is on another level when it comes to being selfless and caring (though I realise I'm a bit biased).

In 2013, when things began to get tricky with my health, we'd only been together just over a year, and we were coming up to the two-year mark when everything went south. Naturally, I wondered if he'd stick around. It wasn't like we were married or even engaged. We hadn't yet made the commitment of 'in sickness and in health', and I honestly wouldn't have blamed my now husband if he'd decided it was too much to take on. I think I even said as much to him, because that's the kind of person I am – I would never want someone to feel obligated to be with me. But he stayed, and not out of obligation. I'm confident of this and thankful every day to have him in my life.

The rest of my family – my parents in particular – were also steadfast in their support during that time. They couldn't fully understand what I was going through and they openly admitted this (so did my husband), but they learned to sense when I wasn't doing so well without me having to say it, and when I communicated that I was struggling, they knew it meant that I was *really* struggling and they would offer me quiet, stoic support. They also never once questioned the genuineness of my illness and symptoms, and they generally allowed me to steer them in terms of what support I did and didn't need, which I appreciated. I say 'generally' because when I started getting out and about again, despite being in my mid-thirties, my parents used to sometimes overstep in that respect. I had to remind them – in a jovial way – that I didn't want to rock up at a social engagement or whatever was planned 'with my mummy and daddy'. But joking aside, I know those missteps came solely from a place of love, care and concern. I'd much rather have had that than people who didn't care and who would leave me to struggle when I did need help. And sometimes I just had to give in and let them look after me.

I know how lucky I was (and still am) with my family, because as well as needing a strong support network, one of the greatest concerns for people with long-term illnesses is finances and financial independence. I'm fortunate enough that I know my husband and family will always look after me, so as long as I have them in my life, I have that security blanket. However, even knowing that, it's still very important to me to have my own income and be able to hold down a job, so that I can retain some financial independence. It's just how I was brought up.

And to be clear, I'm not judging anyone who has to rely on benefits. I feel strongly that the benefits system should be there for those who need it, and I do believe that there's an unfair level of scrutiny on people who are genuinely unwell and unfit for work. When I was trying to rebuild some kind of livelihood for myself – and it really was touch-and-go whether I was fit to work – I signed up for Jobseekers' Allowance, which was a similarly demeaning experience to being dragged through the first stages of the formal absence process in my old job. I felt like a second-rate citizen and like I was under the microscope, and that was even with having a kind and empathetic job coach. The process alone sucked. This is sad, because the last thing people who are struggling need is to be made to feel even more insignificant, powerless and judged than they already do.

Anyway, coming back to my original point, not everyone is as lucky as I am in having a security blanket (even if I don't ever want to have to use it). It really has brought home for me how – unless we're fortunate enough to be rich or have people around us who can offer financial help – we're only ever a few unlucky twists of fate away from a very bad and desperate situation.

One last point I'll cover here is that family doesn't need to be a spouse/partner or blood relatives. I don't buy into the cliché of 'blood is thicker than water' in an absolute sense. I think family can be anyone loyal and dependable who always shows up and provides unconditional support and love. I have a few friends who I could place in that space, even if I don't see much of them anymore. I know they'd be there for me in a heartbeat if I needed them. It doesn't really matter who we consider to be family, what's important is that they're there for us and we're there for them.

Food for thought...

- Who are your family and how do they support you with your illness?

- What do you appreciate about your family and what bothers you about them in relation to your health situation?

- How can you find a better balance if this dynamic isn't working for you? This might include things like more assertively communicating your needs (in a calm and respectful way), thinking differently about the support offered to you or working out what support you do and don't want from your family, so that you can be clear about this with them.

31

You get what I'm saying

Finding connection with others in similar situations

Having a chronic illness can be very lonely and isolating. I've mentioned more than once how I've felt the impact of this. It can seem like you're the only person in the world with the challenges you're facing. But that won't be the case – not in a general sense anyway. The number of people in the UK with at least one long-term condition that impacts their day-to-day life is significant and growing. The coronavirus pandemic resulted in a lot more sick people, whether they have Long Covid or they've suffered the effects of a health system that couldn't help them during that time. Or they may now be stuck on seemingly endless waiting lists for diagnosis and treatment. You only need to do a quick search online to find the headlines that support this. And what it means is there are *a lot* of people across the UK (and the world) who are trying to cope with the impact of significant long-term health issues.

My specific set of life circumstances (health included) is probably quite unique, but I'm not alone in many of the issues and challenges I face and nor are you. I love being around my family and friends. They lift me up and make me feel happy and positive – like I'm LIVING, not just existing – but what they can't do is engage with me at the level of someone who is facing similar struggles. Not in the way that a peer support group can.

For a few years I was an active member of a group that brought together people with different disabilities and long-term conditions. (I'm not going to share the details, because I want to protect the anonymity of those who were also involved.) It was sobering – and in some ways disappointing – to hear the equally challenging stories of the other group members and of the prejudice they faced in their lives, but it was also an uplifting and comforting experience to be part of a community that 'got me'. They understood how I felt and I understood them – not entirely, but there were so many common areas that we really bonded as a group. We also benefitted immensely from learning about each other's experiences and coping mechanisms.

Having had that experience, I don't think it's necessary to interact with people who have my exact condition to benefit from peer support. For me, it's enough to have a connection with others who have experienced the general challenges of long-term illness. In fact, one of the best and most enriching conversations I've had in a long time happened to be at a writers group event, when I ended up sitting next to someone who understood those challenges, and in particular, the stigma and judgement. They weren't the one with the illness, it was their spouse, but they felt that stigma and judgement almost as if they were with living it themselves. And I guess they were because what affects their spouse affects them. We had a great time setting the world to rights together. It was immensely therapeutic.

I did also once take part in an online support group for people with FND. I found it to be an interesting experience because the other participants were describing experiences and feelings that were eerily similar to mine. I did intend to go again, and I can absolutely see the value in doing so, but for whatever reason, I haven't joined a session since. Maybe it just means that I'm at a point with my illness where I'm doing fine and I don't feel I need it right now.

Overall, I guess what I'm trying to say here is there's something magical in meeting kindred spirits. Coming across them in a natural setting is a bonus but seeking out connection with people who might understand things a bit better, and who might be able to offer informed support and advice from their own life experience of long-term illness, can be a very positive thing.

Food for thought...

- How alone do you feel with your illness?

- Who do you have in your life that really understands the challenges you experience?

- If you feel isolated, could you benefit from finding a 'kindred spirit' –

or even a whole group of them – and how might you go about doing this? Charities for different illnesses and diseases often have support groups that they advertise on their websites, or you might be able to find information through your local council.

32

Are you really trying your best?

Learning to live with scepticism and judgement from others

When I was off on long-term sick leave, one of the things I had to demonstrate was that I was doing everything I could to get better. Apparently, this was so that if my employer were to ask for a report from the hospital consultant overseeing my care, they'd be able to confirm that I was, and that would help my 'case' for keeping my job. The reason I've kicked off this chapter in this way is because the question of 'are you really trying hard enough to get better?' didn't just come from my then employer, it also damaged my trust in one of the medical professionals I was supposed to put my faith in to help me get better.

Treatment for FND is limited and so is its effectiveness because there simply hasn't been enough research into the condition to properly understand it. One option available to me was antidepressants, which as I mentioned briefly in my real-life story in Part One, can calm the nervous system response in some patients with FND. But – and it's a very big *but* – they don't work for everyone. I was reluctant to go down this path, and I had good reason for feeling this way.

During my period of overwhelm in my early twenties, I was prescribed antidepressants to help me get back on track. I experienced troublesome side-effects, so it took a couple of tries to find one that I could tolerate and where the benefits outweighed those side-effects. Then, several months later, when I was in a much better place and feeling ready to come off them, the withdrawal symptoms were horrendous. I wasn't told about the possibility of this reaction and was advised to just stop taking them – which I did, and I had no idea what was happening when my body bit back hard. I went back to the doctor who advised me to buy a pill cutter to come off the medication more gradually, but even a reduction of an eighth of a pill at a time was making me extremely unwell. It got to the point where the doctor said I had two options: shave off the tiniest bit at a time, meaning it would take a considerable amount of time to get off the medication, or go 'cold turkey' and ride out the worst of it with Diazepam. No prizes for guessing what I chose (the first option, in case you're wondering), but it took ages and by time I got free of that medication, I'd been on it for far longer than I needed to be.

I considered that experience, and that fact that I'd also experienced a lot of side-effects while on the anti-depressants, to be a good enough reason for being reluctant about taking them again. But apparently it wasn't, and as I've already mentioned, I had phrases like 'nocebo effect' and 'you need to be seen to be doing everything you can to get better' thrown at me. Basically, I was being treated with scepticism and judgement by someone I was supposed to be able to trust to look after my health.

Despite being deeply disappointed by this, I accepted that I should try everything I could to get better and I agreed to take the antidepressants. To say they didn't work for me is a massive understatement. I tried two different types successively (and a third almost a year later) and instead of calming my FND symptoms, each time they sent them into overdrive, incapacitating me and making things worse than they'd ever been. I developed severe breathlessness, huge itchy red hives on my chest and a continuous tremor, which was so severe that I couldn't carry out simple actions like picking things up. At one point, on one of these medications, I couldn't walk at all and fell on my face each time I tried to get up. I had to resort to dragging myself across the floor. I also developed some bizarre symptoms, which included my leg jumping around like it was singularly possessed, and as a passenger in a car my arms would continually shoot up and almost hit the roof in response to unexpected visual stimuli.

If you're laughing at this point, don't feel bad. I did a lot of that myself. I had to for my own sanity, and I really do believe that seeing the funny side of my condition has been a critical part of my recovery.

When I fed all this back to the doctor, they clarified that some patients with functional disorders actually can't tolerate antidepressants – something they didn't tell me at first, probably so that I would give them a fair go, which I did. I simply couldn't continue with them, but I was still treated as if I hadn't given them the 'old college try'.

Now, this sounds bad, and it was, but the sad part is that this is just one example of many. There are great medical professionals out there, and on occasion I've been fortunate enough to be seen by them and receive great care. But too many times, I've been on the receiving end of this kind of behaviour, and it's clear what the people who do this think of me – that I'm an overly anxious and neurotic woman. Well, I'll set the record straight. I'm not. What I have, for whatever reason, is a body that's hypersensitive and this plays out in different ways, which includes a range of allergies and food intolerances as well as drug reactions.

Related to this – and I'm back to talking about my 'scientific study of one', which covers a period of over thirty years, so surely holds *some* legitimacy – I find it very interesting that it only seems to be when a test shows a positive result that I'm believed. I wasn't taken seriously when I had pain in my lower abdomen for months as a child, but when my appendix eventually ruptured, suddenly I was rushed into the operating theatre. I was believed when I said I was having problems with allergies because the blood tests showed a positive result. But I wasn't believed over my recurring respiratory infections until a CT scan confirmed a problem in my sinuses. It shouldn't be that I'm only believed when the 'computer [or whatever testing device is used] says "yes"'. It's also just plain wrong to apply that approach because these tests can't and don't give all the answers. In fact, it seems to me that medicine only has the answers where enough money, resources and open-mindedness has been poured into the research required to find them.

Being treated with scepticism and/or being judged isn't limited to encounters with medical professionals either. I've experienced it both in a work setting and in my personal life – from colleagues, acquaintances, even people I consider to be friends. It can be obvious or very subtle and there isn't necessarily any malintent. We all have biases – that is, that we lean towards a certain set of beliefs or way of thinking – and these biases sneak through in our everyday actions and interactions. For example, one of my biases is towards social equality and people being treated fairly because (for obvious reasons) it's an issue close to my heart. I know I have it, and I consider it to be a good thing overall, but at times I have to reign in the 'activist' within me and try to have an open mind. And especially because it's not always a good idea or appropriate to get on my soap box.

With other people (mainly those I don't know well), what I regularly pick up on is a bias towards thinking my illness isn't as bad as I make it out to be, or that it's something I could overcome with the right diet and/or mindset. Comments like 'Have you tried relaxation/meditation/mindfulness?', 'Sometimes you just need to push yourself', 'Everyone gets tired, it's part of life' and 'Were you a bit anxious or stressed when that happened?' are just a flavour of what I experience. There are also the demeaning comments. I once bumped into an ex-colleague who asked me if I was 'still just working part-time'. She obviously had no idea of the insinuation and impact of her words – she could never understand that managing to work part-time with my condition is an achievement and something I'm proud of – and so I just smiled and answered her question.

Remarks like these are laced with (intentional or unintentional) scepticism and/or judgement, and they're a window into the biases of those who make them. They used to really wind me up, and they do still bother me to an extent – I find it incredible when others seem to think they know more about my illness than I do when I live with it every day – but as they've become a customary part of my life I've been learning to filter them out.

I've realised that I probably need to stop talking about my health situation to people who do the above, but the problem is they often ask how I'm doing and I don't want to say 'fine' in case they take that literally and expect more from me than I can give. Or they take it to mean there's nothing really wrong with me because I 'look well'. It's a no-win situation really. I'm also more than aware of the impact that comments like these have had on me over time. One bad habit I've picked up is apologetic behaviour. Feeling like I'm not believed or not being taken seriously has led to me saying sorry for things I really shouldn't be apologising for (and especially not so profusely) – like not being able to be flexible with social plans, having to go home early because I've run out of steam, being too unwell to work or for needing adjustments at work, for cancelling engagements or appointments at the last minute... the list goes on. I even find myself apologising for inconveniencing others when I have one of my episodes in public (I mean, really?!).

I've got this one on my radar and I need to stamp it out, because I should never have to apologise for not being able to physically cope with something, and

I'm clearly only doing so because, subconsciously, I'm expecting to be judged. Apologetic behaviour with a long-term illness is a thing, though. It's not just me. I've come across many others who do it because of the way society views them, and it saddens me. People who are already having a rough time in life – through no fault of their own – should not be made to feel like their very existence is an inconvenience.

Judgement is everywhere, whether it's an unconscious comment by a well-meaning acquaintance or poorly considered/ignorant and brash statements from public figures about people with long-term illnesses. As I've said throughout, I don't have all the answers and I have areas I know I need to address, but one thing I do know for sure is that I can't change how others behave towards me. I need to be the one to make a change in how I deal with (or avoid providing the opportunity for) these unhelpful comments, so that I can feel more comfortable with how I have to live my life, regardless of what anyone else thinks.

Food for thought...

- What scepticism and judgement do you experience with your illness?

- How does that make you feel and what impact has it had on your thoughts, feelings and behaviours?

- How can you protect yourself from getting badly hurt by bias, ignorance and prejudice? (With this question I'm acknowledging that it will probably always hurt to some extent.)

33

You don't look unwell... oh no, wait...

The challenges of an unpredictable illness

Because of the nature of FND and the relatively low-level symptoms I lived with up until 2014, I've experience of what it's like living as a 'healthy individual' or 'non-disabled person' (if I go with the current recommended terminology). I also know what it's like to be out in the world with both a visible condition and a non-visible condition. And believe me, these experiences are worlds apart. I won't go into the 'healthy/non-disabled' angle, other than to comment that it was a much simpler and easier time. I'm obviously going to focus on the long-term illness side of things.

The title of this chapter (in case you're wondering) is my creative take on the paradoxical moments in my life. What I actually wanted to call it – but it would have been too long – was 'You don't *look* unwell... oh no, wait... *someone call an ambulance*!'. Why? Because that gives a flavour of the nonsensical extremes I've experienced while trying to go about my life outside the four walls of my house. I'll explain.

Many of my symptoms are non-visible, like chronic pain, fatigue, brain fog, sensory issues... it's a long list. They're like invisible assassins that follow me around and try to take me down at every opportunity. When I go food shopping, I can enter the supermarket feeling not bad, but if I stay too long the lights and abundance of visual stimuli send me into a state of sensory overload. This leaves me feeling weak, shaky and sick and no longer coping. My non-visible symptoms also fluctuate (along with my more visible symptoms), which I think makes it even harder for people to understand why I might be able to cope with a certain activity or whatever one day, and then I'll have to rule it out on another. Nobody but my husband (and sometimes my immediate family) sees me on my worst days – and they're *bad*.

When it's just these non-visible symptoms at play, no one would know that I have an illness unless I were to struggle climbing a flight of stairs or I were to tell them about it. In fact, I'm often told how well I look by people who know I have an illness, which I'll admit, does grate on me. Because looking well doesn't mean things are working well in my body.

I guess some of the things I do might mask my illness – but it's not intentional. I wear make-up like most women and why not? I like to look like I've made some kind of effort when I'm out and about. I'm also generally a very positive, smiley and upbeat person who laughs a lot and prefers to just get on with things as best I can. These factors may well create the impression that I'm in good health, making it harder for people to believe that there's something wrong with me. Should I not do these things and instead walk around looking pale and miserable and like it's taken every ounce of my being to drag myself out of bed? All so that my health issues are *believable*? No, I damn well shouldn't. I shouldn't ever have to justify my illness... yet I find myself doing so, over and over.

When I'm just dealing with my non-visible symptoms, people around me will get on with their business and won't give me a second look. This is all fine generally, and in an ideal world, exactly how I would want things to be. But when I'm not doing well, it can become a problem. I might be quite forthcoming about my situation in the natural flow of a conversation, but I'm not good at speaking up – especially in front of strangers – when I'm struggling. This is partly because I don't like inconveniencing people, but also because I'm embarrassed and I don't like drawing attention to myself. For example, busy public transport with no available seating is a *nightmare* for me, because I can't stand stationary for any length of time without becoming weak and shaky and my legs eventually giving way, and motion is a problem because of my sensory issues. It's one of the things I struggle with most when out and about. If I can't find a seat when I need one, things will go downhill fast.

In the past I've tried to ride it out, because I've been too embarrassed to ask someone if they could give me their seat, and it has always turned out badly. Because of this I've learned that it's not worth ending up in a heap on the floor or finding myself stranded, exhausted and fighting to regain control of my body, all because I didn't want to unseat someone who is perfectly able to stand. I've learned that I shouldn't have to pretend I don't have a disability, but it's still not pleasant speaking up. Especially because there are people who regard me with suspicion, as if I'm 'at it'. It's not only in the context of asking for a seat that I feel appraising eyes on me either. It can be in any kind of situation where I need an adjustment made for me or when I sit in seats that are designated for people with disabilities.

Now, I know that some people who read this will doubt my accounts of this. How can I know what others are thinking? I can't read their minds. No, I can't. But I can read facial expressions and body language and I've seen the same cues over and over. These characteristics are a big part of communication and how we show (or expose) ourselves to the world. It almost makes me want to wear a sandwich board that states 'Looking fine doesn't mean feeling fine!'. Obviously, I'm not being serious, not least because I don't like to draw attention to myself, but if you've had similar experiences then I'm sure you'll understand my frustration.

This may sound like enough in itself, but the non-visible aspects of my illness are just one side of the coin. The other, as I already mentioned briefly in Chapter 27, *Shame on you*, in Part Two, is that when my FND becomes visible, it's VISIBLE. It can be anything from noticeable tremors to violent shaking, arms and legs flailing, with muscle spasms in my neck and oesophagus that leave me in agony while coughing and choking. The best term I can use to describe it is a human shitshow. And to clear up any possible misunderstanding, I don't mean that literally (thankfully – but sadly, others may not be that lucky). When these episodes come on, people around me panic, and the first thing I do when I spot that wild look in their eyes is splutter '*Don't... call... an... am-bul-ance!*'. Yes, just like that, because when I'm having one of these episodes I don't have great capacity for speech.

You might be wondering why I have such an aversion to someone calling the emergency services. It's because, as much as what's happening to me looks horrifying and like my life may be at risk (it really does), I genuinely don't need an ambulance, and I don't want to be taking up precious resources that are needed elsewhere. Also, I once received a bill for several hundred euros after an incident abroad because a well-meaning bystander did call an ambulance when they were clearly told I didn't need one – and I refused to get in the damn thing. I certainly don't want that happening again.

The challenges I have while out and about are very personal to me and the way my FND manifests, but what they symbolise is how difficult it is for anyone with a long-term condition to have a life, especially when it means coming into contact with others who either can't see or don't understand what people like me are up against. Oh, how I wish my biggest issues were about what to wear and how to style my hair for a night out. To be LIVING and not just existing, I've made the conscious decision that I will face these challenges, and I'll just have to swallow the discomfort and embarrassment that comes along the way. I've built my own little strategies for dealing with the different scenarios I encounter, and the more I use and improve them, the more confident I become.

Food for thought...

- How much does your illness hold you back from getting out and doing the things you want to do (if you are able to get out and about a bit)?

- What kind of obstacles and challenges do/could you encounter when out and about?

- How can you plan for these things happening and be ready to deal with them when they do?

I think it's important to add here that there's a big difference between pushing yourself a little out of your comfort zone to benefit from a better quality of life and putting yourself in an unbearable or dangerous situation. You must never push yourself to the point that you come to harm.

34

(Not always) a helping hand

People who try to help and get it wrong – and those who get it right

I really don't want this to sound ungrateful; I'm very grateful to anyone who tries to help me during a moment of challenge. The problem is, sometimes others getting involved can be more of a hindrance than a help.

When my body goes into meltdown, my muscles are in spasm, and this seems to include some of those involved in swallowing and regulating my breathing. My eyes also stream, making it look like I'm crying. To an uninformed onlooker it can seem like I'm severely emotionally distressed and having a panic attack when that's not the case. And on multiple occasions I've had people invading my personal space, telling me to 'calm down' and 'breathe', which is very unhelpful indeed. Because in that moment what I really need is space and a way of distracting myself from the worst of the pain and discomfort until the episode passes. (I do also question whether such actions are helpful to a person who *is* having a panic attack, but that's not for me to judge.) So, there's that, and as I mentioned in the last chapter, there's also a tendency for people to overreact when they witness one of my episodes, and that can create even bigger problems for me.

To reinforce my earlier statement, I'm not at all ungrateful for these good Samaritans who want to step in and help, but what it often does is add an extra level of stress and pressure to my situation at a time when I don't need it.

Having read the above, you might be wondering why I don't just politely ask others to leave me in peace – especially if them trying to help causes that much of an issue? If you are, great question. And here's the answer: it's actually harder to do that than you might think when people have shifted into the mindset of dealing with an 'emergency situation'. My preferences can become secondary to them 'ensuring my survival'. It's also difficult to communicate my needs assertively when my power of speech is affected. If I can, I do assert myself and make it clear that I'm OK, but the thing is – much as I hate it – sometimes I really do need help, and I don't always know that from the outset. Like the time when I had an episode on a train shortly before my stop, or when I faceplanted in front of two hundred odd passengers waiting to go through border control at Edinburgh Airport on one of the rare occasions my husband wasn't with me.

I might be off the mark with my thinking here, and what I'm about to share might be uniquely relevant to my condition and specific set of circumstances, but sometimes I think it would be great if there was a broad training of sorts on how to support people experiencing a health episode in public. I know, I know. That's what first aid is all about, but most of the general public don't have those skills. I'm also talking about something much more basic than that – perhaps even just a helpful communication technique for when the person who is unwell knows what they do and don't need. Now, obviously, it's the wise thing not to take risks and an incident should be treated as an emergency if there's any doubt whatsoever – especially if the person concerned is unresponsive or unable to communicate – but in my case, the best thing a bystander can do is take their cues from me and listen to what I need. I will get the words out. Just bear with me while I do so.

All that being said, what I absolutely appreciate is that, even if someone gets things wrong and that creates a negative impact, their intent is always positive. They don't set out to make things worse. They just – understandably – don't have the knowledge and experience to know how best to deal with the situation.

On the day of my nose-dive in front of the border control booth at Edinburgh Airport, I experienced the best example of help I can remember receiving from a stranger. I had been on a flight alone for the first time in several years and it was a particularly unpleasant one. The plane had experienced heavy turbulence during the ascent, the motion of which had set off my muscle spasms and then one of my episodes, then, an hour and a half into the journey, I found myself with an intolerable build-up of pain with no suitable distraction to help me cope. (I'd normally use a film or TV show on a device for this, but I'd forgotten to sort it in advance.) This triggered another of my episodes, but instead of panicking or telling me to calm down, the woman sitting beside me gently engaged me in conversation. This was challenging, because I was having trouble with my speech, but she patiently allowed me the time and space to explain what was happening, that it was something I'm used to and that it would pass. She then asked me if I needed anything and chatted with me through the remainder of the flight, which was an enormous help as it provided the distraction from my symptoms that I needed. It turned out she was in the US armed forces, which made perfect sense – she was clearly trained to assess the situation and keep things calm. She was my good Samaritan that day – she got it just right – and I made sure that she knew how grateful I was.

There's a key lesson I've learned from experiences like this. Much as I feel uncomfortable and a bit embarrassed about it (there's the stigma having its effect), I've accepted that I need to carry my sunflower lanyard wherever I go, just in case I need to whip it out at any point. If you haven't heard of this, it's a way for people to communicate that they have a non-visible disability or condition that others might need to take into account. You can even order a card to attach to the lanyard that says a little bit about your disability/health condition and gives some brief information about your needs.

My condition, of course, became very visible that day on the plane, but there have been plenty of occasions/situations where I've struggled and it's not been so obvious – and wearing the lanyard has helped. Not everyone understands its meaning, but awareness does seem to be growing, particularly in travel hubs and retail outlets. I've also accepted that there are situations where I need to be wearing it from the outset to get additional support, particularly when I'm travelling because, for me, the triggers of motion, sitting or standing for too long and getting overtired are common in these scenarios.

Food for thought...

- What experiences have you had with 'good Samaritans' and how have these helped or hindered you?

- How clear are you about what you do and don't need from others if you find yourself struggling when away from home?

- What could help you feel confident and able to communicate these needs?

35

You're hired

Getting back into the workplace

Back when I had the disappointing realisation that I wasn't going to be able to run a consultancy business and be my own boss, it was time to start looking for a job with a steady income. I won't lie, I felt intimidated by this prospect and not at all hopeful of finding a situation that could work for me. In my story in Part One I mentioned this situation being like 'a big grey cloud looming over me', and that's exactly how it felt. I knew that there was a big difference between working on my own projects and responding to the everyday demands of an employer. Would I even be able to hold down a job? Official paperwork aside, I had left my old job labelled as a 'walking absence problem', and while I had made progress since then, my health was still wildly unpredictable.

The hard truth was that I was living with a broad range of disabling symptoms, there was no sign of that changing, and I had a woefully low level of confidence in my body. That, on top of the fact that I wasn't well enough to work full-time hours, meant I wasn't going to be at the top of anyone's hire list.

The first obstacle I encountered was whether to be up-front about having a disability and my need for part-time hours in my job applications. After chewing over this dilemma, I decided to be open about it. I knew it was a risky strategy and the impact it could have on my job search, but I figured that any employer who didn't want me based on these factors wasn't an employer I wanted to work for anyway. Needless to say, I got quite a few straight-out rejections, and when I contacted a couple of recruitment consultants to see if they could help me, they lost interest the moment I explained my circumstances.

The few interviews that I was invited to were another obstacle. Job interviews are uncomfortable enough, without having to do them with a dysfunctional nervous system. I had always disliked that feeling of being under the microscope

(I mean, who enjoys it really?!), but despite that, I had generally performed well in the past – so I had been told, anyway. However, at that point, the idea of sitting in front of a panel of suited and booted strangers conjuring up awe-inspiring answers that would seal me the offer of a job, felt like a near impossibility. And it almost was in practice. I expect my interviewers would have been none the wiser, but underneath my easy smile and calm demeanour I was begging my ailing body to make it through the experience without humiliating me.

I did make it through those interviews, but I had to rely on notes as a prompt because of my cognitive issues – all of which intensify when I'm under pressure. When I blank in that type of environment there's no glossing over it, so I've learned to cope by being open and bringing some humour to it. However, back then, I just felt too vulnerable to find a funny side. It was also soul destroying to see their interest in me visibly wane as I explained the nature of my health issues.

I think the most frustrating thing about it all was that I knew I could do the jobs I went for and that I would do them well. But only if I didn't end up being dismissed for breaching their absence thresholds. This is actually one of the things that really bugs me about how people with health issues are treated. Governments don't want people on disability benefits, but employers don't want workers they consider to be 'unemployable' because of their health issues (when all it might take is the right adjustments to change that perceived status). With this being the default position, I can see exactly how someone with a similar or worse health situation to mine could fall down that gaping chasm in the middle (and the reality is that I still might if I find myself in a challenging work situation in the future). All it really takes is an employer/manager who lacks flexibility and compassion and things are already heading into a downward spiral. I guess that's why the requirement to make reasonable adjustments exists, but I do wonder how many people with long-term conditions really get the support they need to be in the workplace. The seemingly ever-growing numbers of people with health issues who are out of work certainly doesn't paint an optimistic picture in that respect.

Anyway, back to my job search. It was in May 2016 that I finally got my breakthrough. After reaching out to a few people I knew from previous places I'd worked – those who I thought might still believe in me – I found out about an opening for a temporary role that matched my skillset. When I met the hiring manager at my interview, it felt like someone was looking down favourably on me and finally offering me a break (my mum always says it's my gran – her own mum – who died just weeks before I was born). She was very understanding of my situation and showed genuine compassion, in a way that was respectful, not patronising. It felt like a good match and I could tell (well, I hoped) that she would be willing to provide the working environment and flexibility I needed. Naturally, I was delighted when she saw past my personal situation to my potential, and I was offered the job. It was at a slightly lower level than my previous experience, but that was fine with me – for a while. I needed a way back into the workplace, and I had finally found it.

Many people with chronic illness cannot work at all and that's nothing to be ashamed of. Where others judge, they are the problem. It's a sad fact that the lives of those who already have it tough are made harder by the ignorance and judgement of (some) people who don't know how lucky they are. And for those who are fit to work, but who need adjustments, trying to find a job in a flexible and supportive environment where they're set up for success can feel like searching for the Holy Grail. I've seen glimmers of hope that people with disabilities and long-term health conditions are starting to be treated better than they were a decade or so ago, but it's still a lottery – and that's just not good enough.

Food for thought...

- If you're able to work and you're seeking a job, or your current role isn't working out, what do you need to set you up for success? Think carefully about the type of work you can do and the type of working environment and manager you need to support you. Spending some time thinking about what you need before starting your job search can really pay off.

- What routes have you considered for finding a job? There are now quite a few disability-focused job websites online or you could consider reaching out to a few people you trust like I did.

- How open do you want to be about your situation during the application process? This is very much a personal decision and there is no right or wrong answer. It has to be something you can feel comfortable with.

- If you're unable to work or you're retired, what gives you a sense of purpose?* If you feel like you're lacking purpose in your life, you might find this through a light hobby or interest, learning a new skill, doing an online learning course, or through building connections and making a difference within your community (in whatever way you're able to).

*I covered a bit about this basic human need in Chapter 8, The art of self-discovery, in Part Two.

36

Back in the saddle

Finding my feet again at work

Once I'd cleared the hurdle of getting back on a payroll, my mind shifted from how I was going to find a job to how I was going to keep that job. In the past, starting a new role had been a bit nerve wracking but also exciting. I would have been filled with hope and optimism, keen to make a difference and show my worth. That was all still there, but it was being drowned out by concerns that my body would let me down, and I'd be shown the door before I'd even had a chance to prove that worth. I needed adjustments, and while these had been promised to me, I couldn't help but wonder – based on my previous workplace experience, and despite the positive gut instinct I had when I first met my new manager – whether these were just words and whether they would be backed up by action.

I got lucky. My manager was as good as her word. I'd actually go as far as to say she was a role model and shining example of how a manager of someone with a long-term health condition should be. And no, that doesn't mean she was perfect. She didn't get everything right. How could she? She doesn't live with my condition and she's not a mind reader. But she really tried her best and I could never ask for more than that.

What did she do well? She gave me her time. She communicated with me – and not with a focus on her own agenda, but with my needs and how she could support me at the centre of those conversations. She adhered to the legal requirement to make reasonable adjustments (as per the Equality Act 2010) and stuck to the organisational policy and process, but she used her initiative and did it in a way that made sense for my situation. She treated me like a person and an individual, not a number, and definitely not as a cost to or problem for the organisation. She asked me what I needed adjustments-wise and she went out of her way to make these things happen.

Adjustments do need to be reasonable – as per the legislation – and this is a tricky area because there's no set definition for or concrete list of what's deemed to be reasonable or unreasonable. Expectations can even vary for different organisations because of assumptions around available resources to make changes. There's an obvious problem that arises from that subjectivity. Having worked in HR for a long time and having heard the accounts of people I've interacted with in my personal life, I'm well aware that employees are generally at the mercy of what their manager (or managerial line) deems to be 'reasonable'. Too often, that can be what's convenient for and/or considered acceptable by their own personal standards. To be clear, that's absolutely not how it should be done.

Thankfully my manager wasn't just compassionate, she was pragmatic, and she put her trust in me. She used common sense thinking and realised that if she gave me what I needed, I'd deliver. And she was right. With that vote of confidence, and through feeling like I was valued, I was quickly able to re-build my confidence at work in a safe and supportive environment. I showed that I was good at my job and I delivered more than what was expected of me (something I had a strong track record of doing), which pleased her greatly and hopefully made her glad she had hired me. In fact, one of the best things about how my manager treated me was that, as well as providing the flexibility, support and direction I needed, she treated me like the able professional that I am. She basically gave me the ability, space and confidence to shine – even through my illness.

However, it wasn't all sunshine and roses. My body did let me down and I had some humiliating experiences, which included collapsing and writhing around uncontrollably on the floor and being assisted out of the office to a waiting car. I did have more sickness absence than I would have liked, but it quickly became clear that when I wasn't well enough to make it into the office, I was often still fit to work from home. So, I was granted that flexibility when I needed it – in addition to an existing arrangement we had in place where I worked one day a week from home. Not only did this allow me to keep delivering what was required of me and more, it helped me sustain better physically, because I wasn't overexerting myself when I was further below par than usual.

What the above example demonstrates perfectly is how the question of being 'fit for work' isn't a closed one – the answer isn't always 'yes' or 'no'. My manager understood that it can require trial and error to find the right work set up and that circumstances can evolve. This allowed me to keep offering my best work in a way that also worked for me.

After just under two years in that role, my contract was nearing its end, and I had to start looking for a new job. I didn't want to leave but I needed a secure income, and I managed to find another two-year contract in a different organisation. I won't go into detail but let's just say it was a terrible fit for me, and it became so unbearable that it was starting to undo the positive progress I'd made. I felt trapped and eventually (with the support of my husband) just decided to hand in my notice and try to find something else. By a stroke of luck, within a couple of weeks another temporary role came up in the organisation I had not long left. I threw everything I had into my application and interview, and thankfully, I was successful. I wasn't reporting to the same manager as before, but my new manager was just as flexible, supportive and person-centred in their approach (as were the other managers further up the chain of command) and I thank my lucky stars every day that things turned out that way. I also eventually managed to secure a permanent role in my team, which gave me more financial security.

Since the pandemic I've been working almost entirely from home, and it's made a world of difference to my health and my absence record. Not only am I no longer pushing myself beyond my physical limits on a regular basis, I also haven't had as many colds and viruses – I dislike open plan offices for this very reason. For most people, these respiratory infections are more of an annoyance than anything else, but for me (and I suspect for others like me) they're basically a livelihood killer. Because where someone might just get a runny nose and a sore throat, I often get a full flare-up of my neurological symptoms, which takes longer to pass – and, of course, this can result in me not being well enough to work (though I always try to power through before throwing in the towel). I'd also like to add, because of the debate that goes on around working from home, that I'm much more productive than I ever was in the office, and I've more than proved my worth operating in that way.

I recently took some time out from my job in HR, and contrary to what I expected, I did kind of miss it. It – along with my writing – gives me the sense of purpose that I need. I also enjoy using my skills and making a positive difference through the projects I work on. My career break cemented for me that I want to keep that side of my life going. I really *do* want to work. I want to feel like I'm useful and contributing to society, but it has to be in a way that won't take too much of a toll on my health. I'm doing fewer hours than I was before and I feel like I've finally found the right balance – and the great thing is that I'm still very productive and delivering well. I'm also still writing on my own terms, which is great, because with that side of my life I have much more flexibility. I choose how and when I do it.

My job isn't perfect. No job or working environment is. They all have their frustrations, and I've struggled at times, partly due to my stress tolerance being lower than it used to be. I find it a challenge to sustain throughout the day (even working from home), interactions with others are exhausting (especially when they're difficult) and all the usual workplace frustrations apply. But I know what I have is the absolute best I'll find, and there's no question that it's down to the great mangers I have around me.

Food for thought...

- If you're well enough to work, what's your working life like and how does it make you feel?

- What impact does it have on your health?

- In your job, what helps you and what makes things harder for you? Are you getting the reasonable adjustments you need?

- Remembering that it's important to focus on what you can control, what might help you address some of the things that are having a negative impact on you? This could be anything from thinking about things differently to having a conversation with your manager about barriers (and particularly disability related barriers) that could be removed to allow you to do your job properly.

- How open might your employer be to helping you achieve a better balance in your life to support your health, and what do you think you need from them?

I cannot stress enough how big an impact it has had on me when I've been in a good working environment versus a bad one. I believe that, with the challenge of a long-term illness, it really can be the difference between LIVING and existing. Workplaces that walk the talk when it comes to inclusivity do exist and there are some really understanding, supportive and compassionate managers out there – the challenge is finding them.

Part Four
Some final thoughts

37

A life that I'm LIVING

Where I am now and the life lessons I've learned

I must admit, I've enjoyed writing this book. Not just because I hold great hope of it finding its way into the hands of those who need it most, but because it's been a therapeutic experience. Looking back on the three decades I've spent battling with my health – and particularly the last twelve years – has shown me just how big a challenge I've faced. And I'm still smiling – for the most part. I haven't given up, nor have I allowed my health issues to rule me or destroy my confidence and self-esteem. I've done the best that I can, and under the circumstances I think I've achieved a lot. That's something to be proud of.

I've also learned a lot. About myself, about navigating life during long-term illness and about the world, in the sense of how people like me are viewed. I think that without some of the self-reflection and self-development I've put time and energy into, I might not have fared as well, and I could have found myself in a different place. Staying positive through experiences that could easily have left me feeling useless and fit for nothing has also been key to my 'survival'. And I firmly believe that owning and addressing my problems is an essential strategy for living a life that I can feel good about.

I don't know if it's because my body feels much older than it is or because I'm a future focused person, but I've taken to projecting myself forward as a way of assessing how I'm doing in my life. When I'm at a juncture and I'm not sure how to move forward, or when I'm simply reflecting on how I'm using my time and energy, I often ask myself, 'Will I regret this when I'm eighty?'. It's my way of testing that I'm still on track with living the life I want to live. That way, hopefully, I won't have any regrets when (and if) I do reach that milestone age. I also feel that it's particularly important for me to make the most of the life I have now, because if my FND persists at the same level I know that things will get tougher still as my body ages.

Another thing I've learned is that being self-aware, empathetic and in touch with my emotions are all great strengths. I do occasionally shed tears and this isn't a weakness as I was led to believe for many years. It's a healthy response that will keep me from bottling up unresolved hurt, anger and resentment that could further damage my health or my relationships down the line. Don't sum me up as soft because I'm made of stronger stuff (now more than ever), and in the face of challenges and struggles, I will fight on. I don't know what the future holds with my health, but I do know that whatever it is, I'll deal with it. Knowing that there are many people with the same condition as me who have not been fortunate enough to rehabilitate to the level that I have, and reflecting on my memories of the desperately ill patients in the neurology ward, I'm going to live my life to the fullest I possibly can (within my invisible limits).

I know that I still have areas to work on. I can be a bit of an overthinker (a great strength in creative writing, but unhelpful at times in life), I can be impatient, and at times I push myself too hard. These (very human) flaws aren't particularly helpful, but being aware of them means I can make choices in my life that limit their impact. I'm a big believer in lifelong learning (I mean this in general, not in an academic sense) and I always seek to understand what I can gain from a new experience and how I can improve myself for the future. I've achieved something I never knew I could do – I'm a published author – and through that I've found a whole new sense of self-belief.

I'd say that, despite the ongoing debilitating impact of my FND symptoms, where I am now is in a place of relative peace, taking nothing for granted and making the most of life (as best I can). While I won't lose hope of further improvements in my health, I'm also not going to waste my time waiting to get better. My quality of life may be limited, but it's mine to do what I choose with, albeit within the boundaries of what my body can endure. I know that there are a lot of people in the world who have it much harder than I do, and I'm thankful for what I do still have and the people around me – especially my husband and family. I try to focus on what I can do, not what I can't, and I believe that no matter the situation, if I take responsibility and look for opportunities rather than dwelling on what's going wrong, then I'll come out the other end better than if I don't. Oh, and I'll fall at some hurdles, because like everyone else, I'm not perfect. When that happens, I'll simply pick myself up, dust myself down with some kind words and try again.

What's most important is that I am LIVING, not just existing. And I know that eighty-year-old me is cheering me on.

38

A few final words of support

If you've made it this far, thank you for reading. I hope you've found my ramblings interesting and the *Food for thought* questions of some use. I also hope you feel a little less alone. Sometimes, just knowing there are others out there facing similar challenges who have some understanding of what you're going through can be a comfort.

With a topic as big as this – *improving quality of life during long-term illness* – a quick read and some brief thoughts about how you do things will never be enough if you want to make a meaningful change in your life. So, if you've found this book useful, and you're ready to get in the driver's seat, I'd recommend dipping into it regularly to help you stay focused. It can also act as a support tool when you're stumbling. The chapters and self-reflection questions in Part Two and Part Three are designed to be used in exactly that way.

A quick reminder on two bits of advice I gave earlier. Firstly, don't try and tackle everything at once. That approach won't work. Instead, work through the questions one chapter at a time. Start with the ones that interest you most and/or that are likely to be the easiest areas for you to make gains with. Secondly, remember that your experience of your illness and your set of life circumstances is very personal to you. Make sure you're working to your own motivations and meeting your own needs (and not those of others) as you carve out your path for LIVING with your illness.

Words of advice will come from everywhere – from people who know what they're talking about and people who don't. Filter them in a way that's helpful for you. The same applies to the content of this book. However – and I appreciate how hard this is – try not to fall into the trap of ignoring genuinely helpful advice that you could benefit from, purely because it feels uncomfortable/scary or you think it'll be too difficult (remember Professor Steve Peters' Chimp!). Also, and I can't say this strongly enough, please don't ever push yourself to the point that you're putting your physical and/or mental health at risk. Always consult a trained medical professional if you are in any doubt whatsoever.

Finally, I wish you all the very best with your journey to a better quality of life.

Acknowledgements

This has been my first non-fiction book. It may also be my last – though never say never! What has amazed me about writing it is that it never once felt daunting in the way that writing novels can. I had so much to say that I could barely keep up with the ideas flooding my mind while I did my planning. I also love putting structure around things (that's one part of my day job I love) and to do it with something that was all mine was almost too exciting. And yes, I'm aware of how that sounds, but I don't care. I am who I am, and you know you're onto something special (or at least deeply meaningful) when that happens.

Anyway, getting on with my list of 'thank yous', first up is my amazing husband, James, who features quite a bit in this book. I've thanked him in the acknowledgements of every book I've written and not without good reason. But with this book, it's especially merited. James, you were by my side through it all and without your unwavering support, I wouldn't be able to do half the things I do. You truly are everything to me.

Along the same lines, I'd like to acknowledge my wonderful family, who were also there for me through my most challenging times and who continue to show unconditional support and understanding. As I said in the book, I really have lucked out with you all.

A big thank you to Professor Steve Peters and his team for giving me permission to talk about his book, The Chimp Paradox, which allowed me to bring to life some of my most important personal learnings. Massive gratitude to Fiona Leitch for taking on the role of copy editor and proofreader and heartfelt thanks to Sandy, Elaine, Susie, Fiona, Kathy and Mairi for taking on various roles as beta readers and/or facilitators of my process.

Finally, to my fabulous author friends, Fiona, Sandy and Andie. Thank you as always for your help, guidance and opinions. You know how much I appreciate you.

About the author

Nina Kaye has shared a lot of herself on these pages, which means there's not much to add here. With her fiction writing, Nina has previously published *The Gin Lover's Guide to Dating*, *Take A Moment*, *One Night in Edinburgh*, *Just Like That*, *Stand Up Guy*, *Lucky Number* and *Another Lucky Number*. She has also been a contender for the RNA Joan Hessayon award.